If You Love Me

Spirit Talk
Reverend Paula J Behrens ®
MESSAGES

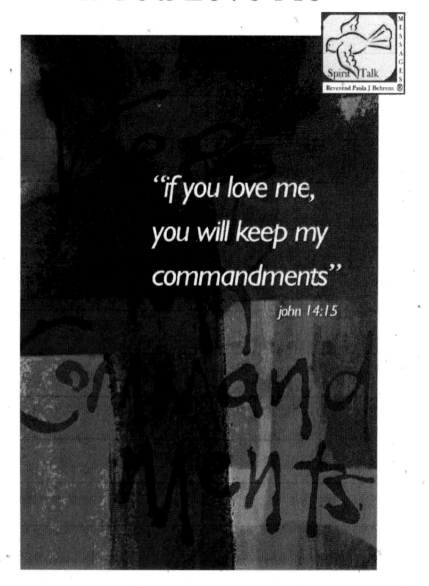

"if you love me,
you will keep my
commandments"

john 14:15

Devotional Messages

January - June 2009

If You Love Me

Other books in the *Spirit Talk collection*:

Walking In the Light
Grace to You
Blessed Are the Peacemakers
Goodness & Mercy
Praise the Name of the Lord
There Is a River

Reverend Paula J Behrens is a full membership Elder in the Texas Annual Conference of the United Methodist Church, Ordained in 2007. She graduated from *Houston Baptist University* with a *Bachelor of Arts* degree in Christianity and English and acquired her *Master of Divinity* from *Perkins School of Theology*, Southern Methodist University.

Reverend Behrens has served as pastor in six United Methodist congregations. She is currently appointed as the Senior Pastor of Chappell Hill United Methodist Church in Chappell Hill, Texas. She has three grown children and three grandchildren. Her desire is to use her gifts and graces in such a way as to bring as much glory to God's kingdom as possible in this lifetime.

Her desire is to use her gifts and graces in such a way as to bring as much glory to God's kingdom as possible in this lifetime.

This collection of messages is lovingly
dedicated to my children:
Sharleen Manning
Bruce Behrens, Jr.
Nicholas Behrens

My siblings:
Cathy Behrens
Bobby Acree
Sylvia Thomas

And the members of:
Chappell Hill United Methodist Church
5195 Church Street/ PO Box 285
Chappell Hill, TX 77426
(979) 836-7795
www.chappellhillumc.org

If You Love Me

Table of Contents

SCRIPTURE INDEX

OLD TESTAMENT

NEW TESTAMENT

Preface

There once was a little girl who attended church only because her parents dropped her and her siblings off for Sunday school and worship every week. Now, this was a good thing, because at least she did have a chance to hear about the love of God. But it was not the best thing, because her parents never joined them for worship and that influenced how she thought about God.

What happened is this little girl grew up thinking that church was only for children. And she reasoned, just as soon as she was grown, well, she wouldn't have to go to church any more. And that's exactly what happened, once she was grown, she did as her parents had done, dropping her own three children off for Sunday school and church, and seldom attending herself. It was her understanding that she was an adult and adults didn't need anyone's help (not even God's). She could and would take care of herself.

She had been taught that if she just worked hard enough, she would be able to get all the things she needed, all the things that would bring happiness and contentment into her life. It might take a while, she thought, but she could do it. And so she worked very hard at acquiring all the things she needed and all the things she wanted, and by the age of forty she had most all of them: a nice house, a faithful husband and three beautiful children.

But guess what, she wasn't happy, she wasn't content. At her dismay, she sensed that there was something missing. She didn't quite know what it was, but she knew something was missing. It seemed that there was this strange emptiness in her life. It was like she had a hole in her heart.

Later she would find out that that is the way our Creator made each of us, with a "God shaped hole" in our hearts. Later she would find out that her life was plagued with a human condition that goes all the way back to the beginning of time. Later she would find in her quest for self sufficiency that she had moved away from the One who created her, that she had become separated from God.

This book, a part of a collection called *Spirit Talk* came about through a little girl's personal journey with God, her journey from unbelief into belief, from something that was less-than-life (as God intended it to be for her) to Life that was "very good" in God's eyes.

Very good, in the first two chapters of Genesis, we hear that it was *"in the beginning that God created"* the world, the cosmos, and everything in it, including human beings, and God saw that it was "very good." We also hear that the first couple (Adam and Eve) walked with God, well that is, until they decided to listen to a crafty old serpent instead. The first couple was given, by God, the ability to make choices, and that day by the tree of "Knowledge and of Good and Evil," they made a not so good choice, which spiritually separated them from the One who had created them. Just like the little girl, the first couple found themselves separated from the One who had created them. They made a choice, and people have been making choices every since that day, some good and some not so good.

For example, there was the prodigal son who chose to leave his father. You might have heard the story. In Luke 15:11-24 there were two sons, one who thought it unfair that his father would throw a party for his irresponsible little brother. And another who was called a prodigal.

According to the dictionary, the word "prodigal" means "recklessly wasteful." It is derived from a Latin word, which is translated "to squander." Therefore, a prodigal son is literally a wasteful son, one who throws away opportunities recklessly and wastefully.

The younger son in this famous parable is a waster. He is one of the most famous wasters in the entire Bible. Now, in our imaginations we can read between the lines and pencil in all the sordid ways he must have wasted his inheritance.

He had a good case of the "give-mes." "Give me the share of the property that will belong to me," he said. He takes the money and blows it on "dissolute living." We know this story well. We know all about this prodigal, this waster. And what we don't know, our imaginations are more than happy to provide.

And we know all about the father, too, who takes back his wayward son even before the confession gets completely confessed. The father runs across the field and smothers his son with hugs, a robe, a ring, and a huge party. But, we have to ask ourselves: Why did the prodigal come back?

Well, he began to feel that emptiness in his heart. He knew that something was missing. He realized that he needed that relationship with his father. The scriptures tell us: *"He came to himself."* You know, it's just a fact that God created us for a living relationship with Him (our heavenly Father). And no matter how much we acquire, or how much we achieve, nothing (can replace that personal relationship with God) nothing can satisfy our soul, nothing, not money, or sex, or power, nothing. God knows that.

Have you ever noticed that the central theme of the Bible is the story of God calling us back into that relationship with Him? It is. Jesus called people to accept the relationship God offers them. In Matthew 11:28 we hear Him saying: *Come to Me, all you who are weary and are carrying heavy burdens, and I will give you rest.*

You see, God offers to us, not a system of rules, but a personal relationship with Him. And with that relationship comes a mysterious and wonderful grace, justifying grace, which begins to work the moment we say "yes" to God. And, our acceptance changes everything. In the story of the prodigal, justifying grace begins when the younger brother turns away from his misery and returns home.

Luke 15: 20-24 says: *So he set off and went to his father. But while he was still far off, his father saw him and was filled with compassion; he ran and put his arms around him and kissed him. And the father said in His joy get the fatted calf and kill it, and let us eat and celebrate; for this son of mine was dead and is alive again; he was lost and is found! And they began to celebrate.* His broken relationship with his father was amazingly restored. And that's what it is like for those of us who believe (but it is even better). Through, belief in Jesus Christ, we are restored to an Eternal relationship with God.

Using the analogy of human courtship, when we accept God's grace, we say "yes" to the One who has been wooing and pursuing us. And as in courtship, saying "yes" changes the nature of the relationship completely. For a husband and wife, saying "yes" marks the beginning point of a lifelong commitment to marriage and a shared life. And this commitment (is meant by God) to resemble our eternal commitment to Jesus Christ and His mission.

But, even though a person responds in faith, it can only be done because of God's grace. The apostle Paul confirms that as he writes in Ephesians 2:8-9: *For by grace you have been saved through faith, and this is not your own doing; it is the gift of God -- not the result of works, so that no one may boast. It is only by grace that you have been saved through faith.*

Another interesting fact about salvation is this. It is instantaneous and continuous (all at the same time). It is correct to say: *I was saved* by grace, *I* am *saved* by grace, and *I will be saved* by grace. In scripture, this spiritual experience of justifying grace is known by several names: salvation, healing, conversion, having one's sins forgiven, or being born again.

And now, as Paul Harvey would say: Here's the rest of the story. The little girl I was telling you about earlier, the one who thought church, was just for children, the one who was on a self sufficient quest for happiness, well that little girl was me. You see, I had chosen the path, the wide path that taught: This life is all there is and you are in charge of making it good. I truly believed that this life was my only chance for happiness. And in my misguided understandings I assumed that after this earthly life, a person just simply ceased to exist.

And because of my childhood experience as a church "drop-off kid," I really didn't even believe that there was a God. And of course if I didn't believe there was a God why in the world would I believe that there was a Heaven or a Hell? It just didn't make sense to me. And so, when you think about all of that, well, it's really not surprising that I didn't come into a saving relationship with Jesus Christ as a child or even as a young adult. The most amazing thing though, is this: God waited patiently, He waited for forty years, for my heart to be ready for the miraculous change that He had in store for His little girl.

I remember it well. I was sitting at the desk in the game room of our 4200 square foot home. And I was feeling that empty feeling in my heart. And I began to pray, really pray, for the first time in my life, I began to pray as though there might just possibly be someone out there to hear me.

I begin by praying: God, if You are really out there, and at that moment God brought back to my memory a verse of scripture that I had learned as a child. It was the verse in Matthew where Jesus says: *Come to Me, all you who are weary and are carrying heavy burdens, and I will give you rest.*

And I said: God, if it is really true that I can have that rest and that peace that Jesus says I can have, I want Him in my heart. I want to give my life to Him. And at that moment my heart was changed.

The way that I saw God, the world around me, other people, and myself was completely different. And as I sat there thinking, I said to myself: Now, I didn't bargain for that. I didn't even know that my heart could or even needed to be changed like that. And then a light bulb came on in my mind.

As the logical thinking person that I am, I realized that I didn't change my heart, but my heart was definitely changed. And I had to ask the question: Well, who did that? If it wasn't me who changed my heart, who did that? Then I realized, that it was something outside of myself that had changed my heart.

And at that moment, I realized that God was real! I began to experience a Joy and Peace and Contentment, like I had never experienced before. I was filled with an unquenchable desire to read the Bible and would do so, two and a half times in the next four months. I also, began to feel a tug on my heart to serve as a pastor in God's church.

Now, I can't tell you that it was easy, no in fact it was quite the opposite, I would say. It was a twelve and a half year journey from call to ordination. But amazingly God was there for me the whole way, strengthening me, encouraging me and carrying me when need be.

And to make a long story short: This *Spirit Talk* collection of books is one small part of my journey with God, one that I wanted to share with you, in hopes that the Lord will take my small offering, multiply it and use it for His glory. And so, here goes. Following you will find a collection of messages that were preached in Chappell Hill, Texas during the first half of 2009. It is my prayer that you might be able to glean a little nugget of God's grace and peace as you incorporate these messages into your walk with Him.

Blessings,
Paula Behrens

A New Vision

Matthew 2:1-12

In the time of King Herod, after Jesus was born in Bethlehem of Judea, wise men from the East came to Jerusalem, asking, "Where is the child who has been born king of the Jews? For we observed his star at its rising, and have come to pay him homage." When King Herod heard this, he was frightened, and all Jerusalem with him; and calling together all the chief priests and scribes of the people, he inquired of them where the Messiah was to be born. They told him, "In Bethlehem of Judea; for so it has been written by the prophet: 'And you, Bethlehem, in the land of Judah, are by no means least among the rulers of Judah; for from you shall come a ruler who is to shepherd my people Israel.'" Then Herod secretly called for the wise men and learned from them the exact time when the star had appeared. Then he sent them to Bethlehem, saying, "Go and search diligently for the child; and when you have found him, bring me word so that I may also go and pay him homage." When they had heard the king, they set out; and there, ahead of them, went the star that they had seen at its rising, until it stopped over the place where the child was. When they saw that the star had stopped, they were overwhelmed with joy. On entering the house, they saw the child with Mary his mother; and they knelt down and paid him homage. Then, opening their treasure chests, they offered him gifts of gold, frankincense, and myrrh. And having been warned in a dream not to return to Herod, they left for their own country by another road.

A family was once driving through Kansas on vacation when their five-year-old son, Tyler, commented: "Wow, it's so flat out there, you can look farther than you can see." "You can look farther than you can see." That's our topic this morning.

Let us pray: May the words of my mouth and the meditations of each of our hearts be acceptable in Your sight, O God, our Rock and our Redeemer. Amen.

In the early 1930's an engineer named Joseph Strauss looked out over San Francisco Bay and in his minds-eye formed a picture of a beautiful bridge connecting the two sides of the bay. In 1936 the Golden Gate Bridge became a reality. Why? Because Strauss had looked farther than he could see.

We know that we need a new vision. Some people look at our healthcare system and cry for a new vision of how to care for the uninsured. Others look at global warming and look for a new vision of how to correct the problem. Many of us long for a new vision that will help to unite us as a people. This vision thing, well, it is so important these days.

Many of us need a new vision for our personal lives, too. Some of us are bogged down in a sea of regret over things we have or have not done. Others of us feel something is missing from our lives. If only we could see something that we haven't seen before.

Vision, if I were to show you a pile of scrap cardboard, old car parts, used tires, and other things of the sort, what would be the first thought to pop into your mind? Trash heap? Junkyard? Eyesore? Probably something like that, yet there is a professor at Auburn University who looks at those same items and can see new homes. Professor Samuel Mockbee is the visionary behind an architecture firm that specializes in making functional, low-cost public buildings and homes for residents in Alabama. Mockbee and his students made these unique, functional buildings out of trash. Specifically, they turned cardboard, old car parts, used tires, and other trash items into real homes. They even built a chapel and community center for the residents of Mason's Bend, a tiny, rural town in Alabama.

Some of the students used more than 100 discarded car windows to make one wall of the center. And other students made homes out of hay bales or old tires. A few of these homes were even attractive enough to be featured in architectural magazines. What happened was this. A group of students learned to see value in what most of us would probably call garbage.[1] Some people look at discarded car windows and see trash. Others see building materials. The difference is vision.

One African American pastor led a thriving church within the community. Asked the secret of his success, the pastor responded: "Well, I hold a crown above each church member and then watch them grow into it." That's the power of vision. Nothing happens without vision. The world hungers for people with vision, for people who choose to look farther than they can see.

In the year 7 B.C. the planets Jupiter and Saturn appeared very close together in the night sky, casting a bright glow similar to that of a single large star. The following year, Mars, Jupiter and Saturn were also closely aligned. Some scholars believe one of these two events produced the bright light in the sky the wise men followed when they came to Bethlehem where Jesus was born. You know the story. But, what fascinates me the most is this: Hundreds of thousands of other people living in the same part of the world saw the bright light in the sky, but they didn't leave their homes to go find the newborn king. What was different about these magi? Vision. It was vision. First of all, the magi were searching for something that was real, something that would transform their lives.

You know, God loves searchers. John Lennon of the Beatles was a searcher. He never completely found what he was looking for, though. He sang a song called: "Imagine." It went like this, "Imagine no possessions; I wonder if you can; no need for greed or hunger; a brotherhood of man."

His radical vision offended many. He envisioned no countries, no religion, no private possessions, nothing to divide people from one another, nothing to fight over or die for, only peace and love and mutual benefit. His was a secular vision rooted strictly in the secular world. The world he envisioned, however, is not that much different from the biblical vision of the kingdom of God, except, of course, Lennon omitted God. How he thought such a perfect world could be produced without God is a mystery to me, because well, humanity on its own volition just cannot produce a perfect world.

But, here's a different kind of vision that is found in the contemporary song: "I Can Only Imagine" by MercyMe. It is a vision of what it would mean to be in God's presence. Our choir sang that song a few Sundays back. You probably remember: "I can only imagine what it will be like when I walk by Your side; I can only imagine what my eyes will see when Your Face is before me! I can only imagine."[2] These two powerful songs, "Imagine" by John Lennon and "I Can Only Imagine" by MercyMe, obviously spring from the word "imagination." Now, imagination is from the word "image," meaning a form or a picture, which comes from the Latin word "imago." And "imago" is derived from the old Semitic root, "mag." Do you see where I am going with this? The old Semitic root, "mag" is the same root word from which the word "magi" originates.

Today is Epiphany. This is the day we celebrate the coming of the magi. Now, you might be saying: What in the world is Epiphany? Well, an epiphany is a new way of seeing or understanding, it's all about a new vision. Like the magi, today is the day we strive to open our minds, and stretch our imaginations. And the first Sunday in 2009, I think, is a good day for expanding our horizons, it's a good time to scan the skies, it's a good time to become searchers.

Did you come searching this morning, or have you found all you need in your new Christmas presents? Your work? Your family? Or a new hobby? Are you so content with the things of this world that you no longer hunger for a fresh encounter with God? You know, God loves searchers. And the wise men, first of all, were searchers. They were searchers who set out on a journey of faith. This is important because there are many journeys that people can take. And because of the ability to choose, some will choose to journey into destructive lifestyles, allowing something other than God to control their lives. Or, maybe they try to be God themselves because they think they have to or because they misunderstand their overall purpose in life. Their vision is cloudy. The fact of the matter is that many people, today, are taking destructive journeys in this world of ours; they're listening to the wrong voice.

A few years back our Air Force built a sophisticated unmanned jet called the Global Hawk. With no pilot aboard, this plane can fly for more than a day, searching terrain and relaying video to a ground station 3000 miles away. A few years back one of these planes was lost in a freak accident. No, it didn't crash into a mountain. It didn't run out of fuel or have one of its parts malfunction. Rather, it committed suicide. It shut its engines down, erased classified material from its computer, set its flaps in a death spiral and smashed at 400 mph into the desert. Here's what happened. More than 100 miles away, a team of Air Force personnel was testing a second Global Hawk aircraft. At some time in this test, this team told this second plane to terminate its flight. Unfortunately, the first plane "overheard" that signal from more than 100 miles away and thought it was being ordered to terminate its flight and it did just that. A forty-five million dollar plane was lost because it listened to the wrong voice.[3]

There are many journeys we can take in today's world, many voices we can listen to, many stars that we can follow. But only one leads us into the path of abundant life. And so, I want to challenge each one of us this year to set out on a new journey of faith by, getting deeper into our relationship with Christ, by joining a Bible study or a Sunday school class, or by spending more time in prayer, or by focusing more intently on God's purpose for our lives, right here in our own community.

My challenge to you today is to see life with new eyes, to see in this world of ours, new and exciting possibilities. The magi came searching for a king and found a new vision. Through Jesus Christ we too, can find a new vision this New Year, a new vision of restored lives. That is if, we are willing to let the power of our Lord flow within, among and through us. What an awesome vision that is, a new vision of healing within our own lives and within our own congregation that is so very powerful that it can't help but flow out into the community around us. A new vision that is what we are seeking for this New Year. Amen.

By Water and the Spirit

Mark 1:4-11

John the baptizer appeared in the wilderness, proclaiming a baptism of repentance for the forgiveness of sins. And people from the whole Judean countryside and all the people of Jerusalem were going out to him, and were baptized by him in the river Jordan, confessing their sins. Now John was clothed with camel's hair, with a leather belt around his waist, and he ate locusts and wild honey. He proclaimed, "The one who is more powerful than I is coming after me; I am not worthy to stoop down and untie the thong of his sandals. I have baptized you with water; but he will baptize you with the Holy Spirit." In those days Jesus came from Nazareth of Galilee and was baptized by John in the Jordan. And just as he was coming up out of the water, he saw the heavens torn apart and the Spirit descending like a dove on him. And a voice came from heaven, "You are my Son, the Beloved; with you I am well pleased."

For each of us there will come times when we need to make choices as to what path we want our lives to take. And that time came for one particular football quarterback[4] during his early days as a pro player. This young man's decisions were influenced by his Christian upbringing. Because of his Christian foundation, he felt God's hand upon his life at a very critical time. When he began to look in the wrong direction God's guiding Spirit helped him to see that He had a plan for his life. He said: *"I knew that God had something better for me."* Being baptized into the faith is very important for us. Because, when we look back on our own baptism we have a starting point, a time when we can say, God had His hand upon my life. Even Jesus felt the hand of His heavenly Father when He was baptized by John in the Jordan.

Mark tells us: Just as He was coming up out of the water, He heard a voice from heaven, saying: *"You are my Son, the Beloved; with You I am well pleased."[5]* Jesus felt the hand of His heavenly Father on His life that day, and when we are baptized in the name of the Father, Son and Holy Spirit, our experience is similar.

Through Baptism we are initiated into Christ's holy Church. We are incorporated into God's mighty acts of salvation and we are given new life through water and the Spirit. This is a gift from God to us. Baptism can be received by a believing adult or an infant. Concerning infant baptism, even before that newly baptized child is aware of what has taken place, he or she is received by the adoptive congregation. That child is nurtured and cared for and loved by the new congregation, not because of anything the child has done or believed, but because the church members have chosen to care for that child. And as the child grows more is expected. And hopefully, at some point the child will come to realize what it means to be a part of the family of God. They mature into a full member, professing their personal faith in Jesus Christ as Lord and Savior.

Have you seen the Disney movie: The Lion King? It's a great movie because it has a lot of symbolism in it when it comes to the Christian faith. For those of you who have seen the movie, you may remember that Simba the lion cub is separated from all that reminds him of his identity. He is away from home, away from his family, and away from his responsibilities in the world. In fact, he forsakes his true identity as the Lion King. And he strays off of the path that had been set in motion when he was baptized a cub. In his absence, the kingdom is over run by forces of evil, and it becomes a very dark and wounded place. The baboon "priest" Rafiki finds Simba in the jungle and calls him to his identity. In John the Baptist fashion Rafiki leads Simba to a lake. As Simba stares into the water, it is not only his face that is reflected, but it's also the face of his father.

The father and son are somehow linked. As he recognizes his father within himself, the heavens open and the father speaks to him, and in that moment, Simba is transformed. He understands his true identity as the Lion King and sees the responsibility his identity carries. He is empowered for the mission that lies before him and, in the end he is victorious and brings light and healing back to his kingdom.[6] Like the little lion cub who was baptized at birth and who had to make a decision to take ownership of his baptism, the newly baptized child of God, no matter what their age, must do the same. But here's the good news. When we are baptized in Christ that means we will be nurtured by God through His Holy Spirit. It doesn't mean we won't stray. It doesn't mean that we are guaranteed salvation. It just means that God is there in a special way, guiding us and calling us back to our true identity in Christ Jesus. If we choose to take ownership of our baptism, through the power of the Holy Spirit we then, experience wholeness and healing and are drawn into a deep relationship with God and His Son.

In baptism the Holy Spirit is called upon, through faith and by the laying on of hands. But the one being baptized still has to claim that power, to reap the benefits of God's kingdom in our lives. That's amazing. Think about this. We who have been baptized have access to the same power that changed timid fishermen into world-traveling preachers. Just as God's Spirit swept across the dark waters of chaos and brought forth light, just as God delivered Israel through the waters of the Red Sea, just as God saved Noah and his family out of the flood, God delivers us through the waters of baptism.

Listen to this true story. Elsie Dewitt was upset when she came into the sanctuary because she wasn't able to sit in her usual pew. Elsie had to sit near the end of the pew, next to the center aisle. She didn't like to sit next to the center aisle especially on Baptism Sunday. She could see at least three families with babies sitting near the front, not far from the baptismal font. No doubt the visitors in her pew were relatives of one of those families.

Elsie had to force herself to come to church on baptism Sundays. She came partly because she didn't know how to explain to her friends why she didn't want to come, but mostly because she could never justify not going to worship. Worship was a joy for her, except on baptism Sundays. She suffered through those, like one might endure the occasional migraine headache. She felt that way because of a secret that she had shared with no one. Her parents had known, of course, but they were long gone. Then it happened. Elsie's heart skipped a beat as the pastor headed her way, carrying one of the babies she had just baptized. It was a custom in the church for the pastor to give each baptized baby to someone in the congregation to hold during the baptismal prayer, as a way of welcoming him or her into the family of God.

"Oh no, it couldn't be," Elsie thought, as the pastor smiled at her and handed her the baby. One of her greatest fears had been realized. Elsie bit her lip and hung on to the baby, trying hard not to let her discomfort show. She breathed a sigh of relief when, at last, the pastor finished the prayer and took the baby back to his parents. The worst was over. But she was still so troubled, that she quietly slipped out of church, before the service ended. That afternoon Elsie called the pastor. She knew that if she didn't share her secret now, she would carry it with her into eternity. She began, saying: "I had a child when I was sixteen. And no one ever found out about the baby. My mother assisted me in the delivery. That all went well enough, but the baby was small, and had difficulty breathing from the first day. I knew I should have had him baptized, but I was afraid of what the pastor might say. So we never sent for him. The baby, died two weeks after he was born. We buried him in the family cemetery on the ridge behind the house. I told my husband about the baby before we were married, but I have never been able to tell anyone about my failure to have him baptized." Then Elsie broke down and wept. Pastor Carol got up, put her arms around her, and held her for a long time.

Finally, Pastor Carol asked Elsie if she would trust her. Elsie said "Yes," and together they made some brief plans for the following Sunday service. The next Sunday Pastor Carol preached on the baptism of Jesus as recorded in Mark's gospel. She talked a lot about God's unconditional love that day. Then, afterwards, she invited Elsie to come forward. Elsie got up from where she was sitting, walked up the aisle, then turned and stood facing the congregation about three feet in front of the baptismal font. Pastor Carol handed her the microphone. Elsie took a deep breath, and then she told them the whole story, just as she had told it to the pastor. When she was finished Pastor Carol took the cover off the baptismal font and invited everyone in the congregation to bow their heads as they prayed. And then, calling Elsie's long lost child by name, she commended him to God.

After that she prayed for the congregation, saying: Pour out your Holy Spirit, so that those who are here baptized may be given new life. Wash away the sin of all those who are cleansed by this water and bring them forth as inheritors of your glorious kingdom. When the prayer was finished, Pastor Carol invited the congregation forward to remember their baptism. They all came. Elsie was the last. Her hands trembled as she lifted them up out of the water. And somewhere from deep inside herself she heard a voice saying: "You, Elsie, are my beloved child."[7]

You see, it is when we open ourselves up to the Lord's baptism that we receive our identity. Elsie received her identity that day. Through her resulting faith she was born anew. And she received the healing grace and power that she needed to be a faithful servant of Christ. We, too, can receive all of this, as we affirm or re-affirm our baptism, and realize who we truly are, forgiven children of God. As a forgiven child of God, Elsie reaffirmed her baptism that day. And we will have that same opportunity in a few moments, on this "Baptism of our Lord" Sunday.

Let us pray:

Gracious and merciful God, we ask that You open our senses to Your presence as we come forward to the baptismal font this morning.

Pour out Your Holy Spirit upon all who come forward this day, forgive us of our wrongdoings, cleanse us of our sins, renew our spirit, and help us to recall our vows as we affirm or reaffirm our faith in Jesus Christ. These things we ask in the holy name of Jesus Christ, our Lord. Amen.

All are invited to come forward at this time. You may dip your hand in the baptismal waters, and remember who you truly are, a forgiven child of God Baptized in the name of the Father and of the Son and of the Holy Spirit. Or if you haven't been baptized, and you would like to be baptized, you may come and sit in this front pew and I will come and talk to you about being baptized. Please come now to receive God's blessings.

The Train Ride

John 1:43-51

The next day Jesus decided to go to Galilee. He found Philip and said to him, "Follow me." Now Philip was from Bethsaida, the city of Andrew and Peter. Philip found Nathanael and said to him, "We have found him about whom Moses in the law and also the prophets wrote, Jesus son of Joseph from Nazareth." Nathanael said to him, "Can anything good come out of Nazareth?" Philip said to him, "Come and see." When Jesus saw Nathanael coming toward him, he said of him, "Here is truly an Israelite in whom there is no deceit!" Nathanael asked him, "Where did you get to know me?" Jesus answered, "I saw you under the fig tree before Philip called you." Nathanael replied, "Rabbi, you are the Son of God! You are the King of Israel!" Jesus answered, "Do you believe because I told you that I saw you under the fig tree? You will see greater things than these." And he said to him, "Very truly, I tell you, you will see heaven opened and the angels of God ascending and descending upon the Son of Man."

Have you been waiting for that certain day or hour, when all the pieces of your life will fit together like a completed jig-saw puzzle? Are you waiting for that perfect moment to get serious about your life of service for God? Have you ever felt like you were on a train ride, just waiting for the right station in life to arrive so you can use your gifts effectively for God? Well, if you have, you need to realize that that station has already arrived. Today is the day to serve God.

Let us pray: May the words of my mouth and the meditations of each of our hearts be acceptable in Your sight, O God, our Rock and our Redeemer.

In our scripture reading we hear of one of Jesus' first disciples who seemed to be looking for that perfect moment. His name was Nathaniel. Nathaniel, better known as Bartholomew,[8] was the fourth disciple. According to John, Jesus called Peter and Andrew first. Then he called Phillip. Then Phillip went and brought Nathaniel.

What do we know about Nathaniel? Well, first we know that he was a person who was waiting and hoping for something. We know that because he was sitting under a fig tree. At a time when people lived in one-room houses, they often planted fig trees out front as a place to "get away." They would sit there to read scripture, or to reflect, or to pray. Sitting under a fig tree was a sign of seeking and searching for something. We also know that Nathaniel was an honorable man, "without deceit" as John puts it. But Nathaniel although he was a good and honorable man, was also an ordinary man. But, that little fact didn't make one bit of difference to Jesus. You see, God has a plan for, well, even ordinary people, like you and me.

Have you ever heard someone say: "I'm only one person. What good can I do?" Well, there's a lot that one person can do. Consider this, Methodism began as a movement of ordinary, individual people, like Nathaniel, who *"came and saw"* and then went out and told others about what was going on in the church. That's how the Methodist church got started. At the beginning of the Wesleyan revival, individual lay people were called to spread the gospel. In Wesley's day, witnessing was the task of the whole church. And that task should be done with enthusiasm, I think Wesley would say.

Here's a good story. There was once a young, brilliant doctor in London who was making a number of experiments in the university laboratory where he taught. He was doing cancer research and his work was supported by some of the most distinguished scientists in London. His workplace was a small, ill-ventilated room in the basement of the university.

The doctor told a friend that if these experiments turned out as successfully as he, hoped they would, then he would have a new way of treating this particular form of cancer. And his friend asked him: "Well, what will you do then?" And with a glow on his face, with enthusiasm in his voice, and a shining gleam in his eye the doctor exclaimed: "I shall tell the world!"[9] Christians who have a glow on their face, enthusiasm in their voice and a shining gleam in their eye, who tell the world about Jesus Christ and His Church, those are the ones who will make the most difference for God.

You know, it is through the lives of ordinary people, that the world will see and hear the story of God's grace. There was once a little girl who had a short line in a church play. All she had to say was, "I am the light of the world." She rehearsed it until she knew it by heart. And as the day drew near she was confident. But, when the little girl saw all of the people the night of the play she became nervous and forgot her line. Her mother, who was seated on the front row, tried to prompt her. Carefully and slowly the mother's lips formed the words: "I am the light of the world." And then, much to her surprise, the little girl's face lit up and she said with enthusiasm: "My mother is the light of the world."[10] And, well, I guess she was right. In a real sense her mother (who was a Christian) was God's light shining in the world. And so are we. Or at least, we can be.

Now, you might be thinking, I can't do that. I'm too old. Or I'm too busy. Or I'm not a leader. But, all God is asking of you is to think about how knowing Christ has changed your life, and then invite others to *"come and see."* The first disciples were all ordinary people, they were followers.

According to John, Jesus called Peter and Andrew first. Then He called Phillip. Then Phillip went and brought Nathaniel. Let's look at Philip for a moment. Why was it so easy for Phillip to bring Nathaniel? Well, because he was watching as others began to place their lives in the hands of this Nazarene.

He listened as Jesus spoke to the people in a way that made them understand their lives better. He saw souls redeemed just as he had seen his own redeemed. So when Phillip asked Nathaniel to *"come and see"* he knew Jesus would redeem him, as well. And so he said to Nathaniel, who was sitting under the fig tree: *"Come and see,"* just come and see for yourself.

Do you believe that God can redeem a soul? Do you believe that He has redeemed your soul? Well, if you do then go out and invite someone else to *"come and see."* Invite them to Sunday school; invite them to worship; invite them to any of our ongoing church activities. Don't be a "Baskin' robin."

Have you heard the story about two robins that were sitting in a tree? "I'm really hungry," said the first one. "Me too," said the second one. "Let's fly down and find some lunch." They flew to the ground and found a freshly plowed field full of worms. They ate and ate and ate and ate 'til they could eat no more. "I'm so full I don't think I can fly back up to the tree," said the one. "Me neither," said the second. "Let's just lay here and bask in the warm sun." "Okay," said the first robin. And they plopped down, basking in the sun. No sooner had they fallen asleep than a big fat cat snuck up behind them and gobbled them up. And as he sat washing his face, he thought, "I love Baskin' robins."[11] Now, here's the question. Will we be people who have eaten so much of God's good food that we only sit and bask? Or, will we invite others. Will we go out of our way to say to someone: *"Come and see?"* That's all I ask, just come and see what's going on in God's church, today.

Wouldn't it be wonderful if each one of us, at least once a month, invited someone new to *"Come and See?"* Wouldn't it be wonderful if *"Come and See"* became a natural part of our lives and our ministry here?

Let me share with you another story. This one is called: "A Man with Two Umbrellas." Dr. Gordon Targerson, a Baptist pastor, was crossing the Atlantic by ship some years ago when he noticed on several occasions a dark-skinned man sitting in a deck chair reading a Bible. One day the pastor sat down beside him and said, "Forgive my curiosity, but I noticed you are a faithful Bible reader. I'd like to visit with you." After introductions, the dark-skinned man said, "I am Filipino. I was born into a good Catholic home. I went to the United States as a young man to study in one of your fine universities, intending to become a lawyer. During my first day on campus, a student dropped by to visit. He welcomed me and offered to help in any way he could. Then he asked where I went to church. I told him I was Catholic. He explained that the Catholic Church was quite a distance away, but he sat down and drew me a map. I thanked him and he left. On the following Sunday morning it was raining. I decided to just skip church. But then there was a knock on my door. There stood my new friend and he was holding two umbrellas. He said that he worried that I might not be able to read the map and so he was there to escort me to the Catholic Church. I got dressed quickly, thinking all the while what an unusually thoughtful person he was. I wondered what church he belonged to. As we walked along I asked him about his church. He said that his church was just around the corner. So, I suggested that we go to his church this Sunday, and then to mine the following Sunday. He agreed. But somehow I felt so much at home in his church that I never got around to finding mine. After four years I felt that God was leading me into, the ministry rather than into law. I went to Drew University's Seminary and was ordained a Methodist pastor. Then I returned home. My name is Valencius, Bishop Valencius, I'm the Bishop of the Methodist Church in the Philippines."[12] Now, the hero of the story is not the Bishop, important though he is. The hero is that anonymous young man with two umbrellas.

Go all the way back to the beginning of Christian history and you'll always find them, that unnamed man or woman with two umbrellas, that person with a winsome faith who builds a bridge of friendship with another person. And across that bridge walks the living Christ to claim another eternal soul.

You know what? You can be that person with two umbrellas. You could say to someone else: *"Come and see."* The fact of the matter is that, God wants to use your life; God wants to use this whole congregation, out in our community and possibly, around the world.

Here's another great story. Church Officers of a certain congregation were debating on whether they should join several other churches in their sponsorship of a local family health clinic. The clinic had been established for the families of migrant workers because the public health resources were inadequate and burdened with red tape. In the debate one of the officers spoke forcefully against supporting the clinic because, as he put it, "Most of the patients are illegal aliens, so we'd just be supporting illegal activity." "But they're people," said one in the group, "and they're already here, said another. It's not like we are bringing them over and they need medical care." Back and forth the discussion went, but with no resolution. So the matter was tabled until the next meeting. The following day, the pastor called the officer who had spoken in opposition and invited him to lunch. After the meal he asked him if he would be willing to take a few minutes to visit the clinic in question. The man agreed, and the two of them found the waiting room at the clinic bustling with activity, full of thoughtful young mothers and their squirming little children. The pastor and the man sat down to observe for a few minutes. A nurse appeared at the door and called to one of the children, a little boy, about four years old, who marched bravely toward the nurse, already rubbing his arm where he knew he would soon receive an inoculation.

A few minutes later the little boy reappeared at the door, now rubbing his arm in earnest, poking his lower lip forward and fighting back tears. He searched the room for his mother, but she had taken his little brother to the restroom and was nowhere to be found. So, the little boy, finding what looked to him like a kind face, walked over to the man who was opposed to supporting the clinic, crawled onto his lap and rested his head on the man's chest. First hesitantly, then willingly and lovingly, the man wrapped his arms around that "little human being" in need of care. And, when he did so, he was amazed by his own spontaneous compassion. And at the next meeting, well, everyone else was just as amazed when he stood up and made the motion that they should sponsor the clinic.[13] It's remarkable what God can do in our hearts as we join in the ministry of His church. You know, it won't be the burdens of today such as, supporting a clinic for migrant workers that will rob us of our joy. But, it could be the regrets of yesterday and the fears of tomorrow, the things we didn't do or the things we were afraid to do that will do just that, that will rob us of our joy. So, let's not waste today looking for that perfect moment to be in service for God.

The true joy of the Christian life is not that of identifying that perfect moment, but it is the trip itself, it is the train ride, it is how we will choose to use our lives saying to others: *"Come and see."* God's purpose is to reach the lost. His purpose will be met. But the question is: "Will we choose to be a part of His purpose?"

Now, some of us have committed to praying for God's guidance over the next few weeks. And it is my hope that as we go to Him in prayer, that as His plan emerges for us, and becomes more clear for us, we will have the courage to make the right choice to embrace His plan enthusiastically, to embrace enthusiastically God's purpose for us here where God has placed us, on this train ride that has brought each of us to Chappell Hill. You are not here by accident. There is a reason God brought you here this morning. And I hope you will spend some time asking Him to make that clear for you today. Amen.

God Has A Vision

<u>Mark 12:28-34</u>
*One of the scribes came near and heard them disputing with one
another, and seeing that he answered them well, he asked him,
"Which commandment is the first of all?" Jesus answered, "The
first is, 'Hear, O Israel: the Lord our God, the Lord is one; you shall
love the Lord your God with all your heart, and with all your soul,
and with all your mind, and with all your strength.' The second is
this, 'You shall love your neighbor as yourself.' There is no other
commandment greater than these." Then the scribe said to him,
"You are right, Teacher; you have truly said that 'he is one, and
besides him there is no other'; and 'to love him with all the heart,
and with all the understanding, and with all the strength,' and 'to
love one's neighbor as oneself,'--this is much more important than
all whole burnt offerings and sacrifices." When Jesus saw that he
answered wisely, he said to him, "You are not far from the
kingdom of God." After that no one dared to ask him any question.*

I read somewhere that a new Guinness World Record had been
set for the world's shortest sermon. It seems that an Episcopal
priest stood up one Sunday morning, walked to the pulpit, stood
there for a moment, and said: "Love." Then he sat down. Now, I
know, some of you would like me to attempt a sermon like that
one day. Oh, come on, admit it.

But, really it's not that easy, because, the word "love" is capable of many different meanings. Love is what a mother gives to her children. Love is what a thrice-divorced Hollywood actress is supposed to have for a five-times divorced actor. Love is what two high school students, parked in an automobile on a lonely road on a dark night are supposed to have. Love is what a soldier, who gives his life for another in wartime, is supposed to have. Love is what God has for us: *"For God so loved the world."*14 You know that passage. Obviously, in each of these cases, "Love" has a different meaning.

In the context of today's Scripture, though, the text points us to Love, as God's vision for us. That's what we will be talking about this morning.

Let us pray: May the words of my mouth and the meditations of each of our hearts be acceptable in Your sight, O God, our Rock and our Redeemer. Amen.

If I ask you, "What does the word vision mean, how would you answer? When we think of the word, vision, we might use it to define the ability to see clearly. For example, we might say: I have 20/20 vision. We also might use the word to describe the power of anticipating that which may come true. For example, someone might say: That man really has a keen vision for making money. And we also might use the word to describe a revelation. The apostle John had such a vision while he was on the Island of Patmos. He had a vision of Jesus Christ and he heard God's message through His angel. So when we use the word vision we may be talking about Eyesight, Insight or discernment.

The Bible gives us God's perception of what our vision should be toward Him, toward ourselves and toward others. Christ declared this plan during His earthly ministry.

First, He said that our allegiance must be directed toward God: *You shall love the Lord your God with all your heart, and with all your soul, and with all your mind, and with all your strength*, He said.[15] That means that we are to put God first in all things. He is to dominate our thoughts, our actions, and our lifestyle, because, if we put other plans or activities ahead of, or in place of God, our vision will become blurred and we will fail as Christians. That's true for us as individuals and it is true for us as a church. You see, we must purpose to glorify God in everything that we do. Our activities must not only be acceptable to God they must glorify Him.

Jesus also teaches us that we must have a true respect for God, for ourselves and for others. After He said that the first commandment was to: *Love the Lord your God with all your heart, and with all your soul, and with all your mind, and with all your strength.* He then said: The second commandment is like it: *You shall love your neighbor the same as you love yourself.*[16] The question though is this: *"Who is my neighbor?"* Who is this person that I am required to love, even as I love myself? And you'll remember that Jesus answered with the parable of the "Good Samaritan" in Luke's Gospel. The moral of the story is that everyone that we come in contact with, who is down in their luck, is our neighbor. We have neighbors all around us. I think Jesus would say, today, that our neighbors are those who may be feeling disconnected, lonely, fearful, or without purpose.

In our church, we come together to worship God. We come as individuals with different backgrounds, different likes and dislikes, different problems, and different personalities. But, in God's house there is something unique that will bring us together, that will bind us together. There is a common thread that will make us one family quicker than anything else, and that is the willingness to serve Jesus Christ, by reaching out to our neighbors in our own community.

One day Jesus told His disciples about the community around them. He said: *Do you not say, "Four months more and then the harvest"? I tell you, open your eyes and look at the fields! They are ripe for harvest. Even now the reaper draws his wages, even now he harvests the crop for eternal life, so that the sower and reaper may be glad together.*[17] The disciples often saw the multitudes that came to Jesus as curiosity seekers, just people looking to see what they might gain. But Jesus always saw them as a part of the valuable harvest and He had compassion on them. He saw them as being loved by God and as potential Kingdom dwellers.

The Harvest, there are some special characteristics of a harvest that we should consider. Perhaps they will help us focus on God's vision for us. First, a harvest is valuable, very, very valuable. The sower plants seeds for a purpose, so that they will grow and produce a crop. This crop is very valuable to the planter. He has invested heavily in the anticipation of a good harvest. God has invested heavily in humanity. He sent His only Son to earth, to die as a sacrifice for the sins of all. That proves to us that every single person, born into this world, is very valuable to God. And a potentially healthy person, who experiences their wholeness because of the trust they have in Jesus Christ is an even greater treasure. Jesus said that if a person possessed the world and all of its wealth, that that value would not amount to the value of even one person who turns their life and will over to Him. Yes, the harvest is very valuable to God.

Second, the harvest must be gathered or it will be lost. When the fruit becomes ripe, it has to be picked. One year, I decided to plant a garden. My tomato vines were full of tomatoes. They had produced what I wanted them to. But when the tomatoes turned red, they were not going to detach themselves from the vine and walk into my kitchen and jump into the salad bowl. No, unless I extended the effort to go out and labor in my garden, unless, I fought the heat and the mosquitoes and picked the tomatoes as they ripened, I would have lost my valuable harvest.

The people who are ready to hear about the healing power of Jesus Christ, the ones God wants to bring into our lives, the ones He wants to bring into this congregation, could be lost if we shrug off our responsibility to tell them about God's grace now while their hearts are ready, which brings us to the third point. There is a great urgency about the harvest. There is a clock running on the harvest. When the fruit gets ripe, when the grain gets golden, there is only a certain amount of time to harvest the crop.

Once that window of time has passed, the opportunity to harvest that particular crop is lost forever. That's why we need to feel an urgency in the mission that God sets before us in these upcoming weeks and months. When God opens a door of opportunity for us, I pray that we will be willing to walk through.

God's vision as, heard in the words of Jesus are to love God, our neighbors, and ourselves. Listen to Reverend John Baker as he describes Celebrate Recovery, a ministry we will continue to pray about over the next two months. He writes: The purpose of this ministry is to fellowship and to celebrate God's healing power in our lives by loving ourselves through the 12 Steps and 8 Recovery Principles. This experience allows us to "be changed" through God's power. We then show love to others by opening the door, by sharing our experiences, our strengths, and our hopes with them. In addition, we become willing to accept God's grace in solving our lives' problems that is, we love God by turning our life and will over to Him. By working and applying Biblical principles, we begin to grow spiritually. We become free from our hurts, habits and hang-ups. This freedom creates peace, serenity, joy, and most importantly, a stronger personal relationship with God, a healthier relationship with ourselves, as well as, with others. Through all of this we discover that our personal, loving and forgiving Higher Power is indeed, Jesus Christ.[18]

This ministry is the essence of following Jesus' commandment to love God, our neighbors, and ourselves, which also lines up with our mission statement, that of "Bringing others to Christ through our Actions, our Words and our Deeds." Action, what would action look like? Well, first going through a healing and wholeness process ourselves would be a good action to take. Why, so that we can be as healthy as possible when we then reach out to share God's love with others.

Words, here's a good example of words: That of inviting the community to come and experience God's healing power and grace in their lives, as well. Saying to those in our community: "You are welcome here. Everyone is welcome here and no one will be judged."

Deeds, there are lots of deeds we could do. Here are a few: Being a leader of a small group, Offering your musical talents as a part of the praise team, Grilling hot dogs or hamburgers or bringing desserts or making coffee for fellowship time, Sharing your own successful experience of a 12 step program, or that of someone close to you. These are just a few ways you could bring others to Christ through your deeds.

Okay, what we have been talking about is the fact that God wants us all to be in ministry. So, let me ask you this question. Do you have a ministry in this church, or is it just a job? There is a difference, you know.

Here are some clues to help you figure out if yours is a job or a ministry: If you are doing something because no one else will, it's a job. If you're doing it to serve the Lord, it's a ministry. If you're doing it just well enough to get by, it's a job. If you're doing it to the best of your ability, it's a ministry. If you'll do it only so long as it doesn't interfere with other areas of your life, it's a job. If you're committed to working it out, even when it means rearranging other plans, it's a ministry.

If you plan on quitting because no one has praised you or thanked you, it's a job. If you stay with it even though no one seems to notice, it's a ministry. If you do it because someone else said that it needs to be done, it's a job. If you are doing it because you are convinced that it needs to be done, it's a ministry. If your concern is success, it's a job. If your concern is faithfulness to God, it's a ministry. It's hard to get excited about a job. It's almost impossible not to get excited about a ministry. People will say "well done" when you do your job. But, the Lord will say "well done" when you complete your ministry. An average church is filled with people doing jobs. But a great church is filled with people involved in ministry. If God calls you to a ministry, for heaven's sake don't treat it like a job. If you have a job, give it up and find a ministry.[19]

Here's something to think about. Our beautiful church facilities were given to us, not for our benefit, but for God's benefit. We have been given this beautiful facility as a tool to help us fulfill God's vision for us. The vision to love Him: *With all our heart, soul, mind and strength and, to love our neighbor the same as we love ourselves.* Making the effort to be as healthy as we can be, as a congregation, and then offering God's healing grace and power to those outside the church, that would be a good start, I think, on fulfilling God's vision. And so, let me just say this. May He fill us with excitement and satisfaction today, as we seek to be, not just an average church, but a great church, striving to fulfill God's purposes for us to the absolute utmost.

Let us pray: Dear God, we ask that You bless and empower us, Your people as we seek to walk firmly in Your will, determined to be obedient to Your plan for us, that we trust will become clear as we continue on this path of fasting and praying for Your guidance. Amen.

Transforming Light

2 Corinthians 3:17-4:6
Now the Lord is the Spirit, and where the Spirit of the Lord is, there is freedom. And all of us, with unveiled faces, seeing the glory of the Lord as though reflected in a mirror, are being transformed into the same image from one degree of glory to another; for this comes from the Lord, the Spirit. Therefore, since it is by God's mercy that we are engaged in this ministry, we do not lose heart. We have renounced the shameful things that one hides; we refuse to practice cunning or to falsify God's word; but by the open statement of the truth we commend ourselves to the conscience of everyone in the sight of God. And even if our gospel is veiled, it is veiled to those who are perishing. In their case the god of this world has blinded the minds of the unbelievers, to keep them from seeing the light of the gospel of the glory of Christ, who is the image of God. For we do not proclaim ourselves; we proclaim Jesus Christ as Lord and ourselves as your slaves for Jesus' sake. For it is the God who said, "Let light shine out of darkness," who has shone in our hearts to give the light of the knowledge of the glory of God in the face of Jesus Christ.

The Apostle Paul wrote: *If the gospel is veiled, it is veiled to those who are perishing, the god of this world has blinded the minds of unbelievers to keep them from seeing the light of the gospel.*[20] Do you remember how lost you really were before you had the Light of Christ? I remember, before I came to know the Lord, I felt that I had made a mess of my life. And I didn't have a clue as to what my purpose should really be. But then, Jesus' Truth was revealed to me, and His Light began to guide me, and amazingly my purpose in life became much clearer.

Each Christian, every person who puts their faith and trust in Jesus, receives the Light of Christ. And with that receiving, comes a great responsibility. Paul wrote: *For we, proclaim Jesus Christ as Lord. And it is God who said: "Let the light of Jesus Christ shine out of darkness."21*

Let us pray: May the words of my mouth and the meditations of each of our hearts be acceptable in Your sight, O God, our Rock and our Redeemer. Amen.

You've probably heard the saying, *"Opportunity only knocks but once."* That saying reminds us of the fact that some occasions will only present themselves once. And when that moment passes, it is gone forever. And so we must ask ourselves: Do I try to seize every good opportunity that God brings my way, or do I sometimes, choose not to?

You can probably think of some opportunities that made a big difference in your life. Opportunities like: Proposing to your spouse; applying for a certain job; accepting a promotion; moving to a new town; or choosing a place of worship. There are probably other opportunities that you didn't take advantage of, too, that would have made a difference in your life. Some, you may be glad you didn't take, but others you may wish you could recall. Paul challenged the church concerning opportunities, saying: *Be very careful, how you live, not as unwise but as wise, making the most of every opportunity.22*

When I think of opportunities, one particular person in the Old Testament comes to mind. In the Book titled "Esther" we find a intriguing story about a Jewish girl who had been given the opportunity of a lifetime. Esther was a pretty Jewish girl whose parents had died when she was very young. Her cousin, Mordecai, raised her. He was from the tribe of Benjamin. And both he and Esther had been carried into exile from Jerusalem by the king of Babylon.

Esther's story took place while King Xerxes reigned in the citadel of Susa. He had just recently gotten rid of his wife, the queen, and was now looking for a new queen to take her place. King Xerxes ordered that the most beautiful girls of his kingdom should be brought to the palace and Esther was among those women. Immediately, Esther won favor in the eyes of everyone who saw her, as well as, the king and he decided that she would be the new queen of Persia. As the story goes, because of an impending danger that Esther's people would be annihilated, her cousin, Mordecai, said to her: *Do not think that because you are in the king's house you alone of all the Jews will escape. For if you remain silent at this time, you and your father's family will perish. And who knows but that you have come to a royal position for such a time as this?*[23]

Esther, in fear of losing her life by going before the king uninvited, decided only after much fasting and prayer to go anyway and plead for the lives of her people. And to make a long story short she found favor in his eyes and he gave an edict, which overruled the previous dispatches. Consequently, the Jewish people were saved. And Mordecai was given a place of high honor in the kingdom.

Esther had been given the opportunity of a lifetime. It could have cost her, her life but she seized the moment and saved her people. You know, you and I are of the royal family of God through Jesus Christ. We have been given a position of responsibility, that of telling others about the Light of Christ. Paul said: *Be very careful, then, how you live, not as unwise but as wise, making the most of every opportunity.*[24]

A word that is often used in church is the word "Revival." We might say we're going to have a "Revival" in October. But what does the word actually mean? Well it means to restore something to its usefulness. It is all about the process of making something valid. It's a restoration to life. It is a quickening, a surge of strength and a return to a life-affirming condition.

In the church we use the word "Revival" in connection with a renewed spiritual condition, a returning to a dynamic relationship with God that once existed. But, revival is always personal before it can become corporate. Revival must start with an individual spiritual change before it can spread into an entire group. Sort of like when we take the Light from the Christ Candle on Christmas Eve and spread that Light to all the other candles in the Sanctuary, until the room becomes very bright.

Do you want to feel God's presence as you once did? Do you want Him to bring revival to your soul? He can. But you must renew your commitment to Him. Do you want to be a faithful servant for Christ? You can. But you must make Him first place in your life. Do you what your life to be a shining Light in this dark world? It can be. It can be, Jesus said: *You are the light of the world. A city built on a hill cannot be hid.*[25]

When I think of all the natural phenomena of our universe, light is the greatest. Have you ever thought of how essential light is? What would our universe be like without stars? What would our world be like without the sun and the moon? Light is extraordinary. It travels as a wave or beam and it illuminates everything in its path. It travels faster than anything else and all molecular movement is limited to the speed of light. Light causes darkness to disappear. What was dark and shadowed becomes completely revealed in the Light. Have you ever been outside on a real dark night when you could not see anything? You immediately realize that you are blind. You become helpless and you have no idea as to what is around you. But if you have a light, the instant you turn it on, it causes the darkness to disappear. Light is extraordinary.

"Let your light shine," Jesus said. Isn't that amazing? Every Christian, having received the Light, has the potential to shine for Jesus. Christ is our light. So, if we truly abide in Him, we WILL reflect His light. Do others see the Transforming Light of Christ in you?

Paul urged the believers in Ephesus to be examples of the Light of Christ. He said: *"For you were once darkness, but now you are light in the Lord. So you should Live as children of light."*[26] *"Let your light shine,"* Jesus said. We have His light within our care, and we have been entrusted with the responsibility to share that Light. That means we are accountable. You and I are accountable to God for sharing the Light of Christ with others. God has a plan for the darkness of this world. And we are here today as a part of His plan.

In our world, today, people need someone to shine His light and they need more than just a little flicker, they need a very bright light, so that the blinders that Satan has placed on them can be removed, literally dispelled by the Light of Christ. Jesus said: *"I am the light of the world. Whoever follows Me will never walk in darkness but will have the light of life."*[27] You know, we were once a people who walked in darkness. We didn't understand. But now we do. Now we do. Now we know that we are the ones appointed, by God, to reflect His transforming light into the community around us.

How well is your light shining? Are you ready for God to shine His "Light of Life" through you today? All I can say is, let us be faithful. That is my prayer for each one of us, today. Let us be faithful. Let us be faithful, Lord. Amen.

He Called Them Friends

<u>John 15:9-17</u>
As the Father has loved me, so I have loved you; abide in my love. If you keep my commandments, you will abide in my love, just as I have kept my Father's commandments and abide in his love. I have said these things to you so that my joy may be in you, and that your joy may be complete. "This is my commandment, that you love one another as I have loved you. No one has greater love than this, to lay down one's life for one's friends. You are my friends if you do what I command you. I do not call you servants any longer, because the servant does not know what the master is doing; but I have called you friends, because I have made known to you everything that I have heard from my Father. You did not choose me but I chose you. And I appointed you to go and bear fruit, fruit that will last, so that the Father will give you whatever you ask him in my name. I am giving you these commands so that you may love one another.

Some years ago in the city of Belfast, a member of a large, church decided to take a religious census among some 2000 area residents. When the results were in, the pastor then found himself seated in front of a huge heap of reports, where he began to note the findings and especially any comments made by visitors at the bottom of the page. One remark that occurred again and again was: "Used to be a Christian; now belong nowhere." Another was: "Our children go to Sunday school, but we aren't interested." And then he found one unusual comment that startled him. It simply read: "Christian, but disconnected."[28] Disconnected, now that's a pretty strong word. It sounds as though somebody has pulled the plug on the poor guy. Or perhaps he has pulled the plug himself.

And that's sad, because God created us to be connected with one another. God intended for us to be in communion with Himself and with one another.

Let us pray: May the words of my mouth and the meditations of each of our hearts be acceptable in Your sight, O God, our Rock and our Redeemer. Amen.

Jesus said: *"I am the vine, you are the branches. Those who abide in Me and I in them bear much fruit, because apart from Me you can do nothing."*[29] Now, these words would have been filled with meaning for those who lived in the first-century Palestine. Vines, and their produce, the fruit of the vine, were and are still a major source of livelihood in the Holy Land. And when Jesus said: "I Am the Vine," He and His disciples had just drunk a cup of the fruit of the vine which symbolized the outpouring of His life. The figure of the vine was everywhere, for them. Often, when they walked to and from the Mount of Olives, they saw vines growing on the hillside. Every time they entered the Temple they saw the symbol of the vine carved upon its gates, for the vine was an ancient symbol of Israel. During the Maccabean period the vine appeared on coins as a symbol of Jewish nationalism. The great prophets of the Old Testament had spoken of Israel as "the vineyard of the Lord."

And it was against the background of these word pictures, that Jesus described Himself as the "True vine." When Jesus called Himself the "True vine," He was making an astonishing claim. He was saying: "I am Israel, the people of God, compressed into one. I am the Servant of the Lord, promised by the prophets of Israel." Jesus was claiming that He was the ultimate disclosure of what God intended for His people to become. They had so often faltered and failed in their mission to the world. But now God had sent into the world the One who would draw unto Himself all of the hopes and the dreams of God's people.

On the eve of His crucifixion, Jesus met with His disciples in the Upper Room, where He shared with them many things. And it was on that eventful night that He conferred upon them the highest honor they could ever receive. He said: *You are my friends ... No longer do I call you servants, for the servant does not know what his master is doing; but I have called you friends.* During Jesus' time, the disciples of a rabbi would have been considered as his servants. But, now, Jesus changes that relationship. He had told His followers all that He had heard from the Father; He called them friends, and He then expected them to pass on to others what He had shared with them.

As Jesus called the disciples in the Upper Room friends, so He calls us friends, as well. And so let me give you a few questions to ponder this morning. First: What kind of relationship do you have with Jesus? Do you picture yourself as a reluctant servant or an intimate friend? You know, how you see yourself speaks volumes about your relationship with Him. And second: Do you do what He commands? Do you know what He wants you to do in this world?

Jesus chose the disciples and appointed them to spread the gospel. Our Lord chooses each believer to be a branch in the vine that bears fruit that will last. Jesus made the first choice, to love and to die for us, to invite us to live with Him forever. We make the next choice, to accept or reject His offer. But, here is the good news for those who choose to accept His offer: We have a friend who loves us, encourages us, strengthens us, and draws forth from us our best qualities.

John G. Paton, a great missionary in the islands of the South Pacific, buried his dearly beloved wife after only three months of service. Left alone, heartbroken, and surrounded by strange and hostile faces, he said: "If it had not been for Christ and His friendship, I should have gone mad and died beside that lonely grave."[30] John G. Paton was a person who experienced Christ's friendship in an extraordinary way.

But here's the good news, for all who choose to accept God's offer: We do have a friend who is closer than a brother, a person who will stand by us especially in times of need and who will never forsake us. But, how can we experience the true friendship of Christ? How can we live with the personal assurance that Jesus is indeed our friend? Well, I think it amounts to three things: Connectedness, bearing fruit, and relying upon God's Power.

But, there is something we all need to get rid of first, and that is pride. Pride, a very common human emotion, is something that will stand between us and God. Pride is that spirit within us that wants to be god, that stubborn belief which thinks we can manage life alone and work out our salvation without God. If Jesus Christ is not your closest and dearest friend, examine your life. Give up whatever is standing between you and Him. For only with Him as your friend, will your lives be exciting, and fulfilling and worth sharing with others.

Jesus called His disciples friends and then He commanded them to be friends to one another. He said: *This is My commandment, that you love one another as I have loved you.* Now in light of that commandment, let's think about a recovery support ministry. The ministry is based on two things, a person's need for God and a person's need for a friend. The individual needs God, and also a friend who has fought a similar battle and found victory, a friend who will stand by them in times of weaknesses, someone who will come and abide with them and bring strength. For anyone recovering from anything, hurts, losses, grief, habits or hang-ups, a part of their victory comes through a continual association with a friend. As long as the individual abides with their friend, the battle can be won. Using this as a model for the Church, can you see what the Church is for? Can you see what Christ intended it to be?

It is supposed to be sort of a "Sinner's Anonymous," not a group of perfect people, not a group of people who have arrived, but rather, people who are willing to be friends, one to another. Jesus said: *This is My commandment, that you love one another as I have loved you. No one has greater love than this, to lay down one's life for one's friends. You are my friends if you do what I command you. I do not call you servants any longer, because the servant does not know what the master is doing; but I have called you friends, because I have made known to you everything that I have heard from My Father. You did not choose Me but I chose you. And I appointed you to go and bear fruit, fruit that will last.*[31] Jesus says that we are connected with Him and with one another. In other words, we are simply not designed to "go it alone" in this world.

John Wesley was right when he said that the New Testament knows of no such thing as a solitary Christian. To be a Christian, is to be connected, to belong to Jesus Christ, and to everyone else who belongs to Jesus Christ. That doesn't mean that an individual cannot have a precious and personal relationship with God, but it does mean that their relationship with God must spill over into their relationships with others. The cross at the center of our sanctuary says it all. One beam of the cross reaches upward to God, while the other reaches outward to others. To be in right relationship with God, according to Jesus, is to be in right relationship with one another, here in God's place of healing.

An outspoken atheist, Charles Bradlaugh, once challenged a preacher named Hugh Price to a public debate in London. The preacher gladly accepted the challenge, but on one condition. He wanted to bring one hundred men and women to the debate who would be witnesses for the redeeming love of God. These men and women would demonstrate for unbelievers how God had turned their lives around. The preacher asked his atheist challenger to do the same thing, to bring one hundred people whose lives were helped by not believing in God.

Well, the debate never took place. The atheist never showed up. And so, Reverend Hughes and the one hundred men and women with him turned that proposed debate into a worship service. One by one these Christians shared the good news that through the power of Jesus Christ and the presence of the Holy Spirit, God had melted their hearts and remolded their lives.[32] In other words, they bore good fruit for their Lord that day.

You know, the emphasis on bearing fruit is sometimes interpreted as a sermon on "doing good works." But that's not the case at all. Bearing good fruit simply means sharing God's love with others, and giving credit to God for the love that flows through you.

James Herriot, a veterinarian in rural Scotland, was once being entertained by a wealthy friend in Beverly Hills, California. His host had a magnificent home with a swimming pool up in the hills. He kept telling Mr. Herriot, though, that in spite of his wealth, and high society experiences, somehow, he "had missed out on life." Later Mr. Herriot commented: "I've stayed put in my little home town, but thank God, I haven't missed out." You see, Mr. Herriot had a different standard by which he judged the usefulness of his life. He knew that his humble service as a rural veterinarian was as noble in the eyes of God as the work of any of his high society friends.[33] Good fruit is not about what we attain in this life, but it's about doing what Jesus calls us, as His friends to do.

And think about this, God is the ultimate judge of what we do with our lives; He is the ultimate judge of the fruit that we bear. It is God, and God alone who decides what will flourish and what is to be thrown into the fire as stubble.

Did you know that bearing fruit does not have to be extravagant? That's true. Anyone who is connected to the Vine can do it. Here are a few things you might consider as you strive to bear fruit for the Lord: Smile more, even to people you don't know. Reach out and touch people, give them a pat on the back or a touch on the shoulder. Look them in the eye. Let them know you are aware they exist. Be concerned about those you work with. Listen when they speak to you. Spend an extra minute. If someone has a problem, just listening means more than you'll ever know. Do all of that and any other act of kindness you can think of, but most importantly, pray every day, at the start of the day preferably, and ask God for the opportunities to communicate to others what the true source of your acts of kindness is.

The heart of the matter is this: Christ is the Vine; that's where the Love originates. And we are the branches; that's where the fruit grows. And when others are receivers of that fruit, they also experience Christ's Love. That's our job. Our job is to be a friend to Christ by being a friend to one another in Christian fellowship and also a friend to those outside the church. Our job is to bear good fruit, to tell others about the Ultimate Source of our fruit and to tell them all He has done for us and all He has done for them too.

Let us pray:
Lord Jesus Christ, we thank You that You are our friend, our guide, and our helper along the way. We thank You that You find us worthy to bear fruit for You. Help us to stay connected, and not disconnected, to You Your people and Your church.

Take from our hearts all pride and vain thoughts that would only give us that feeling that we do not need You. Give us courage to surrender our weaknesses into Your loving hands. And fill our hearts with Your presence so that as You are our friend, we too may be a true friend and bearer of the Good News to those around us. In Your name we pray. Amen.

It Is the Truth That Counts

John 17:1-20
After Jesus had spoken these words, he looked up to heaven and said, "Father, the hour has come; glorify your Son so that the Son may glorify you, since you have given him authority over all people, to give eternal life to all whom you have given him. And this is eternal life, that they may know you, the only true God, and Jesus Christ whom you have sent. I glorified you on earth by finishing the work that you gave me to do. So now, Father, glorify me in your own presence with the glory that I had in your presence before the world existed. "I have made your name known to those whom you gave me from the world. They were yours, and you gave them to me, and they have kept your word. Now they know that everything you have given me is from you; for the words that you gave to me I have given to them, and they have received them and know in truth that I came from you; and they have believed that you sent me. I am asking on their behalf; I am not asking on behalf of the world, but on behalf of those whom you gave me, because they are yours. All mine are yours, and yours are mine; and I have been glorified in them. And now I am no longer in the world, but they are in the world, and I am coming to you. Holy Father, protect them in your name that you have given me, so that they may be one, as we are one. While I was with them, I protected them in your name that you have given me. I guarded them, and not one of them was lost except the one destined to be lost, so that the scripture might be fulfilled. But now I am coming to you, and I speak these things in the world so that they may have my joy made complete in themselves. I have given them your word, and the world has hated them because they do not belong to the world, just as I do not belong to the world. I am not asking you to take them out of the world, but I ask you to protect them from the evil one. They do not belong to the world, just as I do not belong to the world. Sanctify them in the truth; your word is truth. As you have sent me into the world, so I have sent them into the world.

And for their sakes I sanctify myself, so that they also may be sanctified in truth. "I ask not only on behalf of these, but also on behalf of those who will believe in me through their word..."

One day, a woman's red station wagon was crushed, by an elephant at the circus. The owners of the animal apologized, explaining that the animal, for some reason, simply liked to sit on red cars. In spite of the damage, the woman's car was still drivable. So, she headed off to the garage. But on the way, she was stopped short by an accident involving two other cars just ahead of her. When the ambulance arrived a few minutes later the attendants took one look at her car then ran over to assist her. "Oh, I wasn't involved in the accident," she explained. "An elephant sat on my car." And then the ambulance attendants quickly bundled her off to the hospital for possible shock and head injuries.[34] Sometimes it is very difficult to discern the Truth. In His great intercessory prayer, Jesus asks for several things concerning His followers and one of them is Truth.

Let us pray: May the words of my mouth and the meditations of each of our hearts be acceptable in Your sight, O God, our Rock and our Redeemer. Amen.

In His prayer for the disciples, Jesus asks for several things, but He begins by asking for eternal life. He prays: *Father, You have given the Son authority over all people, to give eternal life.*[35] Jesus knows that His "hour" of glorification has arrived and His motives are quite clear. If the Father will glorify the Son through His death and Resurrection, then the Son can, in turn, give Eternal Life.

Jesus asks that the Father restore Him to the divine position for several reasons, I think. First, so that He can more effectively intercede for those who will continue His ministry on this earth. Second, so that they might understand, more fully, the power that the Resurrection holds over death. Third, so that the Holy Spirit can continuously dwell within God's people. And forth, so that believers can receive eternal life.

What is eternal life? Well as seen in this prayer, eternal life is, knowing experientially, God and Jesus Christ. It is being in relationship with the Father and the Son. Jesus says: *This is eternal life, that they may know You, the only true God, and Jesus Christ whom You have sent.* "Eternal life" is being reconciled to the Father and the Son. Every human being needs to be reconciled to God. That's the human condition; we have been separated from God because of sin. And, *"if we say that we have not sinned, we make God a liar."*[36] That's what 1 John tells us.

But, God has a plan for the problem of sin. In essence, God says to us, "Here is my Son, the perfectly obedient one, in whom I am well pleased. He offered a Perfect life, a life totally free from sin and on the cross He prayed for your forgiveness. Because of His perfect obedience, He has the authority to forgive sin. And He has the authority to offer the gift of eternal life." So, God's question to us is: Do you know Him? Do you love Him? If you do then eternal life is yours.

Through this passage we learn that eternal life is something experienced, here and now. But, you might say, I thought eternal life was something promised for the future. That is true. It is promised for the future, but there is also a "here and now" component to eternal life. It is made possible through the indwelling Holy Spirit. And the indwelling Spirit is accessible to those who accept God's plan of salvation, not my plan, not your plan, but God's plan.

Many have tried to devise their own plan of salvation. One misguided group claimed that there is a sort of divinity that is trapped inside the human body, something within that would give us the ability to save ourselves. Another group denied the true humanity of Jesus. They said that Jesus only appeared to be human. This too, is an unacceptable belief, for we hear in 1 John: *By this you know the Spirit of God: every spirit that confesses that Jesus Christ has come in the flesh is from God, and every spirit that does not confess Him as coming in the flesh is not from God.*[37] And then there are those who reject the divinity of Jesus Christ. But the writer of John says: Even though no one has seen God, the Son, who is God, has made Him known to believers.

Okay, so Jesus asks that His true followers, those believing that He is both God and Human, He asks that they have Eternal Life. He also asks that they be protected from evil. He prays: *"Father, protect them, from evil."*[38] In Genesis, the writer says: *"God created humankind in His image, in the image of God He created them; male and female He created them."*[39] But, it was the evil one who came along and tempted the first couple to sin. Jesus knew all about the evil in this world, so He prays that His followers be protected. Jesus asks that His followers receive Eternal Life; He asks that they be protected from the evil one; and He asks that they might have unity of spirit.

Speaking about the importance of unity, Charles E. Jefferson once described the difference between an audience and a church. He said: An audience is a crowd. A church is a family. An audience is a gathering. A church is a fellowship. An audience is a collection. A church is an organism. An audience is a heap of stones. A church is a temple. And he concluded: "Preachers are ordained not to attract an audience, but to build a church." If the Lion's club or the Kiwanis club or any other community group is torn with dissension, it is a shame. But when the church of Jesus Christ is in turmoil, it is a tragedy, because Christ is depending on us.[40] The third request of Jesus is for unity in Spirit, that His followers might have the same kind of oneness that He and the Father enjoyed.

Now, today we see a great diversity within the body of Christ, from person to person, from congregation to congregation and from denomination to denomination. And that is okay, because unity does not mean a blending of all our differences into one homogenized mixture. Unity means that our center is on the one same Lord. Unity means that we share one very important belief, one common foundation, belief in Jesus Christ, God the Son, the One who came in human flesh, to bridge the gap between God and humanity.

The findings of a survey given to eleven major symphony orchestras resulted in this report. The percussionists were viewed as insensitive, unintelligent, and hard-of-hearing, yet fun-loving. String players were seen as arrogant, stuffy, and un-athletic. Other orchestra members overwhelmingly chose "loud" as the primary word to describe the brass players. Woodwind players seemed to be held in the highest esteem described as quiet and meticulous, though a bit egotistical. So the question was: With such widely divergent personalities and perceptions, how could an orchestra ever come together to make such wonderful music? The answer? Regardless of how those musicians viewed each other, they subordinated their feelings and biases to the leadership of the one conductor. Under his guidance, they were able to play beautiful music together.[41] Like individual instrumentalists in a symphony orchestra, diverse as we are, like that, we come together in beautiful music, as the full body of Christ.

Jesus sends up a petition asking that His disciples be one, as the Father and the Son are one. And, finally, He asks that they be Sanctified in the Truth, that they be set-apart by God's Word. "Word," is used in several different ways in the Gospel of John. "Word," to John is Truth. It can mean the written word, or it can refer to Jesus Himself, that is, *the Word who was in the beginning with God and who was God.*[42] What he meant is that, the Living Word brings "light" and "life" to God's people, reconciling them to the Father.[43]

Knowing the Truth, experientially, brings life now for: It is the Truth that forms God's people into one body; it is the Truth found in God's Word and effected through the power of God's Spirit, that brings us together in unity, that makes us one; it is the Truth that makes "knowing God" possible. Jesus said: *"I am the Way and the Truth and the Life; no one comes to the Father except through Me."*[44] Jesus is the Truth. He is the Way that leads to Life with the Father. He is God the Son. Now sometimes when we share that with the secular world, it wants to bundle us up and send us off to the hospital to see if we might be suffering from possible shock or head injuries. But, that doesn't make the truth any less the Truth.

Jesus and the Father cannot be divided. If you come to the Father you also come to the Son, and vice-versa; it's not possible to come to one without coming to the other.

Jesus is the One who brings us into Eternal Life: It is because of the Truth (Jesus Christ) that we have Eternal Life, it is because of the Truth (Jesus Christ), that we are protected from the evil one; it is because of the Truth (Jesus Christ) that we are delivered from sin and death; it is because of the Truth (Jesus Christ), that we are molded into the one body of believers. Even in all of our diversity, as long as Jesus Christ is our center, we have unity in Him, and are sanctified by Him to continue His work in this world.

And here is the best part. After Jesus prays for His future followers, Jesus speaks to God on our behalf. We are those who have believed through their word. Jesus places our future squarely in the hands of the Father. The Son, tenderly, asks that the Father will be present in the life and mission of this faith community, in the life and mission of Chappell Hill United Methodist Church. He has already placed us under the Father's protective care and loving-kindness. And He was bold enough to hold God the Father accountable.

You have sent Me to them, He says. *You have given them to Me. You have loved them,* He says: Now give to them Eternal Life, keep them safe from the evil one, let them be one, and sanctify them in the Truth which is Your Word, who was made flesh to walk among them."

Jesus prayed for us. We have His words right here in front of us, That is absolutely amazing, absolutely amazing. So, you see, it is the Truth that counts. Our future is in the hands of God and, because of that, "we can do all things through Christ who gives us strength."[45] So be it, in the name of the Father and of the Son and of the Holy Spirit. Amen.

Empowered

Acts 2:1-21

When the day of Pentecost had come, they were all together in one place. And suddenly from heaven there came a sound like the rush of a violent wind, and it filled the entire house where they were sitting. Divided tongues, as of fire, appeared among them, and a tongue rested on each of them. All of them were filled with the Holy Spirit and began to speak in other languages, as the Spirit gave them ability. Now there were devout Jews from every nation under heaven living in Jerusalem. And at this sound the crowd gathered and was bewildered, because each one heard them speaking in the native language of each. Amazed and astonished, they asked, "Are not all these who are speaking Galileans? And how is it that we hear, each of us, in our own native language? Parthians, Medes, Elamites, and residents of Mesopotamia, Judea and Cappadocia, Pontus and Asia, Phrygia and Pamphylia, Egypt and the parts of Libya belonging to Cyrene, and visitors from Rome, both Jews and proselytes, Cretans and Arabs--in our own languages we hear them speaking about God's deeds of power." All were amazed and perplexed, saying to one another, "What does this mean?" But others sneered and said, "They are filled with new wine." But Peter, standing with the eleven, raised his voice and addressed them, "Men of Judea and all who live in Jerusalem, let this be known to you, and listen to what I say. Indeed, these are not drunk, as you suppose, for it is only nine o'clock in the morning. No, this is what was spoken through the prophet Joel: 'In the last days it will be, God declares, that I will pour out my Spirit upon all flesh, and your sons and your daughters shall prophesy, and your young men shall see visions, and your old men shall dream dreams. Even upon my slaves, both men and women, in those days I will pour out my Spirit; and they shall prophesy. And I will show portents in the heaven above and signs on the earth below, blood, and fire, and smoky mist. The sun shall be turned to darkness and the moon to blood, before the coming of the Lord's great and glorious day. Then everyone who calls on the name of the Lord shall be saved.'

A pastor in New Hampshire tells about a birthday card he sent his dad. It was his father's 75th birthday and Kinsey was looking for "that perfect card." Standing there in the card shop, his eyes kept going back to one card, one that had a drawing of two boats tied to a dock in what appeared to be a New England town. Although Kinsey lives in New England, his parents live in the hills of West Virginia. His parents had never owned a boat or even showed any interest in boating, but, Kinsey continued to look at the card. There was something about it that was meaningful. You see, Kinsey describes his father as a very simple man, He believes in simplicity. His style is uncomplicated. As Kinsey continued to look at the card, he noticed that one boat was a sailboat, the other a rowboat. He wondered. If his father had to make the choice, which boat would he choose? Kinsey bought the card, and in a note to his Dad shared the thoughts he had in the card shop. Then he asked his father this question: "Which boat would you choose?" Several weeks later, he received a response from his father. He wrote: "I noticed that the rowboat had no engine, but that the sailboat had a sail. So my question is this: Is there any wind?"[46]

Our reading today is about the Day of Pentecost, the birthday of the church. And the question we will be asking is: Is there any wind? Are we bound to spend the rest of our days rowing, dependent on our own power alone? Or is there a way we might put our sails up so that the wind of God can catch us?

Let us pray: May the words of my mouth and the meditations of each of our hearts be acceptable in Your sight, O God, our Rock and our Redeemer. Amen.

The most exciting changes ever witnessed in a group of human beings happened two thousand years ago on the day of Pentecost. Pentecost literally means "50." It was an annual Jewish festival that took place fifty days after another Jewish festival called Passover. It was mandatory that all Jews living within twenty miles of Jerusalem attend the Pentecost festival. Thousands of other Jews from neighboring countries flocked to Jerusalem for this happy occasion. So, the city was packed with over a half-million people, as it is described in the second chapter of Acts. And on the day of Pentecost about 120 followers of Jesus gathered in an upper room. They were excited and expectant because they had seen the risen Christ. The day of Pentecost was a life transforming experience for them. And they would talk about it for the rest of their lives. On that day the sound of a violent wind suddenly filled the house and indeed the surrounding area, like that of a hurricane or a tornado.

In Hebrew the word for wind and spirit is the same, *"Ruach."* That mighty wind of the Spirit blew into the church and with it came an inrushing of confidence, faith, and joy. And the disciples, there, saw divided tongues as of fire flickering above each one of them. You see, three years earlier, John the Baptist had predicted: *"One mightier than I is coming. He will baptize you with the Holy Spirit and with fire."* Fire has a way of burning away the chaff. And it also has a way of refining and galvanizing whatever it touches. The hearts of the disciples were refined that day; they were set on fire, with love for Christ, and an overwhelming desire to tell the story.

Do you know what the official symbol of the United Methodist Church is? It's a Pentecostal flame and a cross. Our mission then, is to tell and live a cross-centered life, empowered and illumined by the Holy Spirit. And it was John Wesley who said: "The renewal of the soul, after the image of God can never be wrought in us except by the power of the Holy Spirit."

On the day of Pentecost the disciples thrust open the closed doors they had been hiding behind. They poured out into the streets where a crowd was. And then, enabled by the Spirit they spoke in languages of all the foreigners in the crowd, that day. And so, each person heard a special delivery message in his or her own language.

Just consider these changes that Pentecost made in the disciples: The fearful became fearless. Facing the very same Jewish Council which had condemned Jesus, Peter indicted them all for executing the Messiah. And when the Council warned the disciples not to teach in His name, Peter replied: "*We must obey God rather than men.*" The disciples now refused to be intimidated. When Peter and John were beaten within an inch of their lives, what did they do? They rejoiced over the privilege of suffering for Christ. The amplified Bible says: "*They were dignified by the indignity.*" The disciples who earlier had been silent began to shout the good news. When persecution forced them out of Jerusalem, they told the story over an even wider area. The power of the Holy Spirit gave the first disciples' the courage they needed to go out and spread the message.

A great missionary to India[47] was fond of saying: "Without the Holy Spirit, I'm a mess. But, with the Holy Spirit I'm a message." At Pentecost God entrusted the Gospel to a group of people, so obviously under qualified that anybody with any common sense at all, would know that the Power had to have come from God. And so, my challenge to us today is to dare to live a Pentecostal life-style. And how does one do that?

Well, first, we ask each day for a fresh infilling of the Holy Spirit. In Ephesians, chapter 5, verse 18, Paul issues this command: "*Be filled with the Spirit.*" Those who are filled with the Holy Spirit are those who crave it and are willing to change anything the Lord requires so as to serve Him as He commands.

We should never ever try to live a single day without being refueled by Almighty God. A few years ago in the Rose Bowl Parade in Pasadena, a float stalled. Frustration increased quickly because other floats couldn't pass by on this nationally televised event. Mechanics quickly surveyed the stalled float, searching for the problem. Finally, someone had the presence of mind to check for fuel, only to find that it was out of gas. This became even more embarrassing when the crowd realized that the float's sponsor was one of the major oil companies.

Embarrassingly, sometimes Christians find that their gas tank is empty. But it doesn't have to be that way. The power available to every Christian far exceeds any fossil fuel, or even nuclear energy. The Holy Spirit is the greatest power in our universe. Remember to ask for a daily in-filling of it.

And, a second challenge, if we would live the Pentecostal life style would be to share our experiences of the Holy Spirit with each other in church. A few years ago at Annual Conference, Reverend James Moore shared a story about, a time when he had suggested to his congregation that they participate in a program called "Four Weeks of Love." The first week, the church members were to make phone calls to other members. The second week they were to write letters. The third week they were to make visits and the fourth week they were to invite one another to the next Sunday's worship service. Well, after Dr. Moore's message was over, one man came up to him and said: "Pastor, you know that I love you and that I love the church, but I just can't participate in this program. It's just too syrupy for me." And Dr. Moore said, "That's okay. I understand. You don't have to participate if you don't want to." But a strange thing happened the following Sunday. That same man came up after the service and said: "Dr. Moore, I want to apologize for what I said last week. I was totally out of line and I think the 'Four Weeks of Love' is a great idea."

Well, a little confuse Dr. Moore asked: "What happened to change your mind?" And the man simply patted his suit pocket and said: "I received one of those letters. And I carry it in my pocket and take it out several times a day to read it. Because that one person took the time to write me a letter, well, I know that I am loved," he said. "And the knowledge that I am loved has changed my life forever."

As we share with each other the love of God and what the Spirit has been doing in our lives, we strengthen and help each other to grow. When's the last time you shared with another church member what the Spirit has been doing in your life?

A third challenge, if we would live the Pentecostal Life style is to live over our head. In other words, if you are not attempting something that you could not possibly achieve without God's help, then your aim is too low.

Did you hear the story of the two caterpillars who were crawling along? They looked up and saw a beautiful butterfly fluttering around. And one caterpillar said to the other: "Charlie, you'll never get me up in one of those things." God wants us to live over our head, borne on the wings of the Spirit. There are miracles God wants us to witness. There are scars He wants to remove, ministries He wants us to discover and fractured relationships He wants to restore. The question is: Do you have enough faith to take on something that looks impossible?

And finally, a fourth challenge, if you would live a Pentecostal Life style is to give God the glory. Make it a habit to tell people that you're living on borrowed power. Then when they ask, tell them where the power comes from. That's what the first disciples did. Notice what they told the people on the day of Pentecost. They weren't discussing their own credentials. They were proclaiming God's mighty acts.

One writer[48] was asked some time ago: "What is the hope of the United Methodist Church?" And the answer was: "The hope of the United Methodist Church is the Holy Spirit." God and God alone can save a soul, transform a life, change a city, and renew a denomination. Therefore, we need to always rely upon His power, and then give Him the glory.

About five years ago when I heard that God was sending me to East Texas, I was serving as an associate pastor in Houston. And when I first arrived there, only one couple in the congregation knew of me previously, but I wasn't afraid. Why? Because back in 1999, in my first appointment as senior pastor and then again in 2001, I had begun to learn what it meant to be borne on the wings of the Spirit. God taught me that if He sends me somewhere, He will always pack my suitcase with all that I will need to serve Him. And as I am well into my second year here in Chappell Hill, I can also look back and say: Yes, this has been a glorious experience in God's sufficiency, too. God has inclined you to be amazingly kind and supportive of me, actually He has allowed you to spoil me. And God has allowed me to feel comfortable as your pastor and spiritual leader. And even though I know that I could never live up to all the tasks that God sets before me, that doesn't really matter, because God equips me to do all that He calls me to. Because, you see, God can do extraordinary things even with ordinary people like me, and you too. And with that in mind, I dare you to live a Pentecostal life style.

Don't be content with a powerless, ho hum, life-style. Tell God that you want to soar on the wings of His Spirit. Because, when you will do that, His awesome Pentecostal Power will then, be manifested in ways that go far beyond what you could ever dream.

And so I say, rely on God and His power to help you fulfill His calling on your life of service today. Rely on Him, everyday, call on the power of God's Spirit in all things that you do. Don't be afraid to put your sails up so that the wind of God can catch you. Amen.

Radical Hospitality Imitates Christ

Luke 7:36-47

One of the Pharisees asked Jesus to eat with him, and he went into the Pharisee's house and took his place at the table. And a woman in the city, who was a sinner, having learned that he was eating in the Pharisee's house, brought an alabaster jar of ointment. She stood behind him at his feet, weeping, and began to bathe his feet with her tears and to dry them with her hair. Then she continued kissing his feet and anointing them with the ointment. Now when the Pharisee who had invited him saw it, he said to himself, "If this man were a prophet, he would have known who and what kind of woman this is who is touching him--that she is a sinner." Jesus spoke up and said to him, "Simon, I have something to say to you." "Teacher," he replied, "Speak." "A certain creditor had two debtors; one owed five hundred denarii, and the other fifty. When they could not pay, he canceled the debts for both of them. Now which of them will love him more?" Simon answered, "I suppose the one for whom he canceled the greater debt." And Jesus said to him, "You have judged rightly." Then turning toward the woman, he said to Simon, "Do you see this woman? I entered your house; you gave me no water for my feet, but she has bathed my feet with her tears and dried them with her hair. You gave me no kiss, but from the time I came in she has not stopped kissing my feet. You did not anoint my head with oil, but she has anointed my feet with ointment. Therefore, I tell you, her sins, which were many, have been forgiven; hence she has shown great love. But the one to whom little is forgiven, loves little."

Maybe you've heard the story about a pastor who was having difficulty with his assigned parking space in the church parking lot. It seemed that people parked in his spot whenever they pleased, even though there was a sign that clearly said: "This space reserved." He thought the sign needed to be more, clear so he had a different sign made, which read: "Reserved for Pastor Only." Still people ignored it and parked in his space whenever they felt like it. Maybe the sign should be more forceful, he thought. So he devised a more intimidating one, which announced: "Thou shalt not park here." That sign didn't make any difference either. Finally, he hit upon the words that worked; in fact, almost no one ever took his parking place again. The sign read: "The one who parks here preaches on Sunday!"

I tell you this story because most, not all, but most of you would probably shy away from the prospect of preaching on Sunday morning. But that doesn't mean you don't have a ministry here. For you see, there are a variety of ministries in which all the people of a church can be involved. And today we will be talking about a ministry everyone, I think, can participate in, the ministry of hospitality.

This morning's message on hospitality will be the first in a five-week series on the practices of fruitful congregations, as found in Bishop Schnase's book. And there are a several ways that you can invest yourself in this series. You could get a copy of Bishop Schnase's book and read it on your own, or you could pick up a copy of the devotional book *Cultivating Fruitfulness* and read it each day during the Lenten season. You could also, participate in our Lunch Bunch study immediately following worship each of the five Sundays. And because, God calls each of us to be active participants in the body of Christ, I hope you will pick out at least one or two of these activities to participate in during the Lenten season, which is a time when we ask God to prepare our hearts for Easter.

Let us pray: May the words of my mouth and the meditations of each of our hearts be acceptable in Your sight, O God, our Rock and our Redeemer. Amen.

There is a contemporary Christian music group called Casting Crowns. You may have heard of them. And they have a song out that I really do like. It is called: "If We are the Body." The song begins by talking about a young woman who tries to slip into a worship service unnoticed, but some girls in the back pew tease her with their laughter. Then a traveler, sitting on the back row and is "greeted" by judgmental glances. And finally comes the first piercing question of the chorus: But if we are the Body why aren't His arms reaching?

Now, each and every one of us would want to be treated hospitably, but that is not always the case, as we drive down the highway, as we shop at the local grocery store, as we finish up a busy day at the office and sometimes even as we sit in a church pew, we are not always treated hospitably. But, from the days of Abraham, through the admonitions of the Old Testament prophets and throughout the ministry of Jesus, and finally into the dawning of the early church, radical hospitality was always important to God. It was a practice that God expected of His people. Unfortunately, hospitality was not always offered in times of need, with the outcome of difficult and sometimes even disastrous results for the traveler. In fact, Jesus Himself, encountered less than hospitable behavior in the home of Simon the Pharisee, as we heard in our reading this morning. And, I think we can even say that Simon's behavior actually revealed more than rudeness. I think that it probably resulted because of hostility that Simon had toward Jesus, which, I am sure, would not have gone unnoticed by Simon's other guests. On the contrary, Jesus always practiced radical hospitality. While He rightfully could have claimed some kind of special status, He never treated one person in a more preferred way than He treated another.

In fact, He associated with people who others ignored. He even welcomed little children who, in that culture, were often considered a nuisance. Yes, Jesus showed hospitality to all people. He welcomed all people and He still does that today. So, as His church, we need to do the same. Makes sense, doesn't it? And to that, Robert Schnase, writes: Following Jesus' example of gathering people into the Body of Christ, inviting them to the banquet of God's gracious love requires intentional focus on those outside the community of faith. Jesus' example demands an unceasingly invitational posture that we are to carry with us into our world of work and leisure, and into our practice of neighborliness and community service.[49]

You see, hospitality is not simply something we do, it is an attitude. It is our posture as a church. And that is so important. Because, as Schnase points out: "People are searching for churches that make them feel welcomed and loved and needed and accepted."[50]

Radical hospitality also means that we do not get to decide who will receive our welcome. The last verse of "If We Are the Body" reminds us that the price Jesus paid on the cross was too high for us to be able to pick and choose who will be allowed in. And if, indeed, we are the body of Christ, then we must welcome everyone, just as Christ welcomes everyone. Our neighbor is not only the nice person who lives next door to us, but also, the person with whom we are in tension, as well as, the person who doesn't even like us. In the parable of the Good Samaritan,[51] Jesus forever defined who Christians are to embrace as neighbor.

And Paul echoes the same sentiment when He writes to the church at Rome, saying: *Bless those who persecute you; bless and do not curse them. Rejoice with those who rejoice, weep with those who weep. Live in harmony with one another; do not be haughty, but associate with the lowly; do not claim to be wiser than you are. Do not repay anyone evil for evil, but take thought for what is noble in the sight of all. If it is possible, so far as it depends on you, live peaceably with all, if your enemies are hungry, feed them; if they are thirsty, give them something to drink. Do not be overcome by evil, but overcome evil with good.*[52] If we are the body, we through the power of Christ must be willing to practice radical hospitality. We must imitate Jesus, that is, if we are the body.

You know, Jesus' life and ministry was a gift. He took the loaves and the fish and fed the multitudes. He told a story about a dinner party and the invitation to guests, some who responded and some who did not. In His life and in His relationships, Jesus was always reaching out to others. At times some would complain about this. They had the idea that the righteous associated with others who were righteous, that the clean ate with those who were clean and did not associate with those who were unclean. And Jesus had to remind them: *"It is not the healthy who need a doctor, but the sick,"* and *"the son of man came to seek and save what was lost."*

And so, we will sit down together at a meal in just a few moments where God will say: "My Son, Jesus, will preside. And He will eat not only with the worthy people, but also, with the unworthy, not only with the righteous, but also, with sinners, not only with the faithful, but also, with the unfaithful, not only with the older brother who has done everything right, but also with the prodigal son who has done everything wrong. And when we come we will not presume to come to the Lord's Table trusting in our own righteousness, but in the manifold and great mercies of our Lord.

And we will understand that while we, too, are not worthy so much as to gather up the crumbs under the table, our Lord is the same Lord, who has mercy upon us and who welcomes us, even us, into His presence. What a great and glorious God we serve. Charles Wesley expressed that as he wrote: Come, sinners to the gospel feast; let every soul be Jesus' guest; ye need not one be left behind; for our Lord has bid all humankind[53]

Let us pray: Gracious Jesus, as You have so welcomed us to Your table, help us to welcome others. As You have offered hospitality to strangers, help us to be hospitable to people we do not know. As You have associated with all those in need, help us to be willing to reach out our hands to all people, as well, remembering that You love them, and so should we love them; remembering that You died for them, and so should we live for them, all for Your honor and glory. Amen.

Seeing the Lord

Isaiah 6:1-8

In the year that King Uzziah died, I saw the Lord sitting on a throne, high and lofty; and the hem of his robe filled the temple. Seraphs were in attendance above him; each had six wings: with two they covered their faces, and with two they covered their feet, and with two they flew. And one called to another and said: "Holy, holy, holy is the LORD of hosts; the whole earth is full of his glory." The pivots on the thresholds shook at the voices of those who called, and the house filled with smoke. And I said: "Woe is me! I am lost, for I am a man of unclean lips, and I live among a people of unclean lips; yet my eyes have seen the King, the LORD of hosts!" Then one of the seraphs flew to me, holding a live coal that had been taken from the altar with a pair of tongs. The seraph touched my mouth with it and said: "Now that this has touched your lips, your guilt has departed and your sin is blotted out. " Then I heard the voice of the Lord saying, "Whom shall I send, and who will go for us?" And I said, "Here am I; send me!"

Do you remember the Smothers Brothers? Well, one of their routines on TV went something like this. Dick asked: "What's wrong, Tommy? You seem despondent." Tom replied: "I am! I'm worried about the state of America." Dick said: "Well, what bothers you about it? Are you worried about poverty and hunger?" "Oh, no, that really doesn't bother me." "I see. Well, are you concerned about the possibility of war?" "No, that's not a worry of mine." "Are you upset over the use of illegal drugs by our young people?" "No, that doesn't bother me very much."

Looking puzzled, Dick asked: "Well, Tom, if you're not bothered by poverty or hunger or war or drugs, what are you worried about?" And Tommy replied: "I'm worried about a lack of concern."

A lack of concern is a problem in our society, today, but passion on the other hand, is valued in many areas of life. The passion we have for sports in our society has made many people quite wealthy. Whether it is college basketball's March Madness or the World Series or the Super Bowl, people watch the game while jumping up and down on the couch or screaming and yelling in sports bars adorned in their team colors. Some die-hard male fans actually paint their chest with their favorite player's number, and alternately stand and sit, for three hours in an open-air stadium in sub-zero temperatures. In other realms of life, we believe that healthy romantic relationships involve passion, and that good salespeople are passionate to make a big sale. Some are passionate about their hobbies and leisure activities, like playing golf or going fishing or something else. And anyone who wants to find passionate young people need only to attend a popular music concert. Individuals will vote for passionate politicians, listen to passionate preachers, watch passionate actors, and follow passionate leaders. The fact of the matter is, we are all attracted to the passionate. But, what does it mean when we put the word "passionate" in front of the term "worship?" Well, that's our topic for this morning.

Let us pray: May the words of my mouth and the meditations of each of our hearts be acceptable in Your sight, O God, our Rock and our Redeemer. Amen.

John Wesley, the founder of Methodism, was a passionate preacher of the 18th century who led worship services characterized by passion. So, does that mean that the people would jump on the pews and roll in the aisles, well no not necessarily, but Wesley does note in his journal that periodic "swooning" took place during some of the gatherings.

The passionate worship of Wesley's time was founded on the belief that God was indeed doing something significant in their midst, and thus there was an anticipation, a readiness to hear a word from the Lord, to be prepared for the Spirit to move in unexpected ways. In response to that, they sang their hymns with great joy and they prayed earnestly. Wesley was known for passionately proclaiming the Gospel and there was no doubt he did believe what he was preaching especially in his post-Aldersgate days.

It was indeed the case that early Protestant Christians were passionate worshipers, but something happened along the way. Christian worship lost its passion, I think, when people began to gather, not in gratitude to God, but in anticipation of receiving something from God. Because, you see, worship is not about us, it's about God. In worship we read Scripture to remind us that the main actor in the biblical drama is the Lord. The same is true of our worship. Without gratitude, we will gather for the sole purpose of receiving from God, rather than giving glory to God. We become like an ungrateful child on Christmas morning who, after opening up the many presents, wonders why there aren't more gifts under the tree.

Now, don't get me wrong, we do receive in worship, but that is the result of our giving. For, we find that as we worship with glad and generous hearts, giving thanks for God's amazing grace, then He, who cannot help but be generous toward His children, will indeed give to us in worship the word we need. But what we receive is the "icing on the cake." It is not the fiber of worship itself. God-centered worshipers do not go to church wondering what they will get in return for their time on Sunday morning. Instead, they enter the sanctuary anticipating the same kind of experience the prophet Isaiah had when he saw the Lord high and lifted up. Passionate worship, whether it is traditional or contemporary, is always marked by joy and gratitude.

When worship is not joyful, when it does not reflect a deep gratitude toward God, then it becomes primarily about us. It's not the style or the music or the flow of the service that makes worship boring, but it's when worship is no longer about God, the One who makes all things new, the One who transforms all of life.

There was once an ad in Time magazine that asked the question: "Is God keeping you from going to church?" The ad read something like: "Maybe you are uncomfortable with the idea of God, or at least with someone else's idea of God. Yet maybe you yearn for a loving spiritual community where you can be inspired and encouraged as you search for your own truth and meaning." Now, they called themselves a church, but I would lean towards identifying them as merely a religious institution. Because true worship is not about searching for truth and meaning inside of us, but instead it is about searching for the Truth that can only be found outside of us, that is God. God is the Truth that every soul longs for.

Isaiah understood something new about worship, that day in the temple. He understood for the first time, perhaps, that worship is not about habit. We don't come to worship out of habit or obligation. If we do, we come for the wrong reason. We don't come to worship to be entertained. We don't come to worship for the performance. Now it's okay at times to applaud what happens in a worship service. But before we put our hands together, we need to stop and ask: "Who am I applauding?" If we are applauding Jesus Christ and God Almighty, that's a good thing. But those who are up here to help with worship aren't doing it for their glory. So don't applaud for their performance, rather applaud because they have moved you to a new level of your appreciation for your love of God and Jesus Christ, or because they have helped you move to a new place in worship. Applause is a good thing at times. Then there are other times when the best response is simply to quietly sink into the moment that has been created for you by God through what someone presents as an offering.

Getting back to our text, Isaiah helps us to understand three things about worship. First, worship is about seeing the Lord. It is not about anything that has to do with us. It is not about fellowship. It is not something we do out of habit. It is not a performance. No instead, worship is an encounter with God. Passionate Worship is the kind of worship that takes us to a new place where we can see God differently than we have ever seen God before. But Isaiah's problem is the same as ours. This type of worship can't be described. He has done the best he could using human language to portray the experience he had that day in the temple. His words come out of apocalyptic literature, which is writing that says: I don't know how to describe this. It is beyond anything that words could ever say.

So, let me use the only words I have to try to help you understand how powerful this was in my life. Yet these words will always fall short. Some of you in here might be able to identify with Isaiah. Sometimes the experience is so deep that it can only be expressed in the form of weeping. Isaiah sees angels; he sees the temple filled with smoke; he sees God in a way he had never seen God before. He sees the Lord and says: "In the year King Uzziah died," which is very specific. In other words Isaiah is saying: In the year 740 B.C. I saw the Lord in the temple, and it made a difference in my life. The bottom line concerning worship is this: When we come to worship, we need to center down and focus on the real reasons we are here, we need to focus on our purpose in worship.

We are in the presence of the Almighty as a community of faith. It is like that sense of awe and wonder you get when you walk down a street in the midst of a big city. You might look up and say: My goodness, how did anyone build that? Or perhaps you are awe-struck by a beautiful cathedral or other architectural marvel. Structure can bring that out in us. The works of God are even more awe-inspiring. Just drive around in the countryside some evening and look at the scenery. How beautiful it is. You experience a sense of awe at the beauty you see.

Or maybe you're in the mountains or on a beautiful ocean drive. Wrap all of that up, all the feeling you have ever had about structures, about nature, or even about people whose awesome character captures your attention, and it doesn't even come close to the awe, wonder, reverence and adoration we experience when we worship together, when we really worship together.

When we center down on who God is in our lives, just as Isaiah did, we can't even begin to tell someone what is happening to us as we worship. Centering in worship is not only an individual thing, it's a community affair. This is a place where we gather together so that God can hear us as one voice. There is a sense of togetherness, a sense of unity that God creates among us when we worship together and it moves us to a place where our time alone, our quite time with the Lord in private worship, becomes much more powerful. Or maybe they are not so quiet, yet whether we praise God privately in quiet worship or not-so-quiet worship, it is in community that our worship is centered. And it all spreads out from there.

Isaiah essentially says: I saw the Lord differently than I have ever seen Him before. And because of that, Isaiah sees himself very differently too. And he says: Oh, I am in trouble. I am doomed, for I am a sinful person who lives among sinful people. But the good news is this: It is God's angel who acts and brings the coal to cleanse Isaiah's lips, the very lips that just said they were sinful lips. Isaiah is purged by the grace of God in worship. And it is in worship that we too, discover God loves us anyway, and we encounter God in a new way. God comes to us and begins to cleanse us and change us and transform us into the people we are meant to be. That is, in Passionate worship we move closer to God's image. And then, God says: Okay I have these needs in my Kingdom. I need someone to go. Who am I going to ask to go? And the same prophet Isaiah, who just two verses before was saying: I am doomed, now stands on his own two feet, looks face-to-face with God and says: Here am I, Lord. Send me.

Worship is the encounter we have with God and the consequences that result from that encounter. When we worship passionately, we see God and understand "who God is" differently than we ever have before. We open ourselves up to God, discovering in the process that God is opening us. We allow ourselves to be open and we see differently. We see God differently, we see others differently, we see the world differently and we see ourselves differently. And through all of that our soul is stirred in a way that only God can stir it. We encounter God and come to know how much God loves us. And we wait to see what God is going to do in our lives with these words ready on our lips: Here am I Lord, send me! That's what Passionate Worship is about.

Let us pray:
Dear God, we wait in these moments, in these days, in these weeks to see what You want to do in our lives. And as we wait, we do so with glad and grateful hearts, striving to offer to You our very best. Each week in this time together may we lift to You the worship You deserve. May we sing, pray, preach and meditate in reverence and passion, gratitude and grace, so that You may be high and lifted up in our midst. In the name of Your Son and our Savior, we pray. Amen.

Learning to Soar

<u>Ephesians 3:14-21</u>
For this reason I bow my knees before the Father, from whom every family in heaven and on earth takes its name.I pray that, according to the riches of his glory, he may grant that you may be strengthened in your inner being with power through his Spirit, and that Christ may dwell in your hearts through faith, as you are being rooted and grounded in love. I pray that you may have the power to comprehend, with all the saints, what is the breadth and length and height and depth, and to know the love of Christ that surpasses knowledge, so that you may be filled with all the fullness of God. Now to him who by the power at work within us is able to accomplish abundantly far more than all we can ask or imagine, to him be glory in the church and in Christ Jesus to all generations, forever and ever. Amen.

Gallup Research is a wonderful organization that has done a lot of research related to churches. And a recent poll was surprising, in that it stated that 80 percent of Evangelicals shared that their faith really made no real difference in their lives. That was surprising to me. And the only thing I can figure out is that somehow this 80 percent must not have continued to develop their faith. They don't have a complete picture of the fullness of the Christian life. Somehow they have dropped out of the Christian community.

It's sort of like the duck who flew south each winter with a great flock. And one year he decided to make a stop along the way. He dropped out of the flock and down into a barnyard where there were a lot of chickens. There he discovered the most astounding thing. He could eat all the feed he wanted. Life was really good, and he could just kind of check out. So he stayed there while his friends continued south. Well, when it came time for his friends to fly back north again, he thought about going with them, but, no, he liked the barnyard. It was a pretty good life and he thought he had everything he needed. The next year when the flock came by on its way south, he thought: Maybe this time I'll go with them. So he took a big running start. But guess what? He couldn't get off the ground. And he thought to himself: I don't think I am a duck anymore, because I can't even fly.

How many of us can be compared to that duck? Things are pretty good; all we have to do is stick around. We don't have to fly, we don't have to work and grow in our faith. We can just keep coasting along. But, you know what? We need to understand that we can be among the 20 percent who are still growing. We need to know that there is more to faith than just believing that something is true. We need to know that God has more for Christians who want to grow and soar in their faith.

Here's a story about a Prince in Grenada who was an heir to the throne in Spain. The story goes like this: At a certain time, there were people in control who decided to put this particular Prince in prison. And he was placed in solitary confinement with only one thing to read: the Bible. So, he read it over and over again. Then after 33 years he died and when they came to clean out his cell, they found some notes he had written on the soft stones of the prison walls. He knew that Psalm 118:8 was the verse in the very middle of the Bible. He knew that Ezra 7:21 contained all the letters of the alphabet but "j". He knew that Esther 8:9 was the longest verse in the Bible. And he knew that there were no words in the Bible having more than six syllables.

But, do you think that just knowing the Bible was enough? Well, the Apostle Paul thought not. He wrote in Ephesians 3 that a person must also have faith. Knowledge of the scriptures alone is not enough.

John Wesley was an Oxford Don. And once when he was invited to preach at Oxford, he preached a sermon titled: "The Almost Christian." He got in the faces, so to speak, of those intellectual giants at Oxford and told them they had so much knowledge that they had lost what the truth was really about, Jesus Christ. He called them "Almost Christians." And do you know what their response was? Well, they banned him from all the churches of England. So, Wesley began to preach in the fields, and the Methodist movement was born. It swept across England and came to our country, growing into the Methodism we have today. This all happened because Wesley decided to state the truth, that there is more to faith than just head knowledge, that true faith requires more than simply our human ability to reason.

Now, reason is a good thing. Wesley would agree with that, in fact it is one of the four parts of his Quadrilateral for understanding truth and faith. God gave us a mind for a reason, to use it, Wesley would say. But our reasoning will only take us so far. We must step beyond, by learning to grow in our faith. The problem is that, at some point, many Christians begin to think that they are mature. They begin to think that classes and groups where a person can grow in their faith are only for those other people, those who still need to grow. They don't need that anymore, they tell themselves. They're comfortable where they are. They think they are mature Christians. But, you know what, there is nothing more dangerous in the Christian walk than to claim to be a mature Christian, because the more a person grows in their faith, the more they realize how far they still have to go. Growing in faith, sanctification, becoming holy, becoming Christ-like, is a process that goes on throughout our entire lives. From the beginning to the end, we are to experience more and more and more of Christ in our lives.

Or as CS Lewis put it: "We have to begin again every day, understanding that each morning is a new day for learning what God wants us to learn." And when we realize that we begin to ask questions like: God, what are You going to teach me today? Where are You going to take me today? How are You going to show me Yourself? How are You going to use me, so that I might grow in my faith?

This is faith. Faith is the understanding that we have to start over every day, that every day is a new beginning of our journey with God. And you know what else? Many of us don't realize that it is actually the Holy Spirit who stirs in us the desire for more of this kind of faith. We don't conjure up more faith for ourselves. No, instead, it is a free gift that God offers each of us each day. And so, "O God, give me more faith" should be our plea when we wake up every morning.

Now, if you are here in worship this morning because you had a yearning to be here, well, that is because God stirred deep within you that desire. But the yearning doesn't stop there. God also stirs within us a desire for more, more of who God is. God leads us to want to be more Christ-like. God moves us to a point where we want to become part of a small group where we can fellowship together, worship together, support one another, pray together, share our burdens together, and then serve together.

That's what small group ministry is about. It is a place where we can grow in our faith, even more so than in worship. Worship lights our fire. Being in a small group keeps the fire burning and makes it stronger. For, it is in a small group, that the fire begins to grow. That's what happened in the Wesleyan movement. Wesley discovered that it was when they met in small groups that their faith began to grow.

Now, you may be in a small group and still feel that your faith is not growing as quickly as you would like. Well, that's okay too. Listen to this. Twentieth century archaeologist uncovered some interesting things about the ancient Temple Mount in Jerusalem, one of which is the seemingly random design of the southern stairs. It was by these stairs that weary travelers climbed several hundred feet from the valley to the actual Temple. The rise of the steps varied in some instances by several inches. Now, some might conclude that the design engineers were incompetent, but the ancient rabbis saw the random, sometimes risky state of the southern stairs as a powerful metaphor for intentional faith development. They argued that those who would approach God must do so with intention, caution and measured steps, paying attention to learning along the way.

In our own faith development, we sometimes find ourselves growing by leaps and bounds, while at other times we may actually feel as though we are stuck on the same step way too long. But I would argue that every aspect of our journey, no matter how big or small carries us, closer to the goal of living like Jesus. The key is in taking the journey with care and intentionality. Each step, no matter how deep or shallow, is an important step in a persons' journey toward sanctification.

Now, Jesus not only calls us to grow in our faith, but He also calls us to live our faith. We are to become, literally, a living faith. We are to be people who become more and more like Jesus. And in that process, we become the hands and feet of Christ. But we need to understand that we do not do this on our own, it is God through His Holy Spirit who empowers us. God is the One who moves us along by faith. The goal, I think, of intentional faith development is to allow God's Spirit to create us anew so that we carry with authenticity the image of our righteous and holy God. It is choosing to open ourselves to God's Word and to God's will.

And so, if you are not presently part of a small group whose purpose is intentional faith development and support, I encourage you to take that step today. Make a commitment to be a part of the many and various groups we currently have now, or plan to have in the near future. When we finally realize that this Christian journey is not one to be traveled alone and we decide to be a part of a small group, God then gives to us a place and an opportunity to grow in our Christian walk. And that growing place, the small group, will take us to the point where we're not stuck in the muck of a barnyard anymore. It will give us the ability to rise up to where we are soaring with the best, with other Christians who are being moved from one level of faith to the next, as God takes His church to a higher calling. And because of a holy boldness that comes from growing in our faith, we will reach the place where we want to fly. And we will discover that we can do it, not through our own strength, but through God's strength.

And so, in conclusion: For us to be able to soar as God would have us to soar, we need to each have an intentional plan in place. God's part in it, no doubt, is already intentional. But the question I place before us today is this: Is our part intentional? Are we ducks or are we chickens? Are we satisfied with the barnyard, or do we long to feed on the faith that Christ offers to us, when we intentionally do what needs to be done, so as to be equipped to be among God's best, all for God's glory? Intentional faith development, by every single member, that is what is required of God's people, if we want to grow to be more and more like Christ.

Let us pray: Lord, our prayer today is: Get us out of the barnyard and help us to fly again. We pray in Your name. Amen.

Risky Business

Philippians 3:1-14

Finally, my brothers and sisters, rejoice in the Lord. To write the same things to you is not troublesome to me, and for you it is a safeguard. Beware of the dogs, beware of the evil workers, beware of those who mutilate the flesh! For it is we who are the circumcision, who worship in the Spirit of God and boast in Christ Jesus and have no confidence in the flesh-- even though I, too, have reason for confidence in the flesh. If anyone else has reason to be confident in the flesh, I have more: circumcised on the eighth day, a member of the people of Israel, of the tribe of Benjamin, a Hebrew born of Hebrews; as to the law, a Pharisee; as to zeal, a persecutor of the church; as to righteousness under the law, blameless. Yet whatever gains I had, these I have come to regard as loss because of Christ. More than that, I regard everything as loss because of the surpassing value of knowing Christ Jesus my Lord. For his sake I have suffered the loss of all things, and I regard them as rubbish, in order that I may gain Christ and be found in him, not having a righteousness of my own that comes from the law, but one that comes through faith in Christ, the righteousness from God based on faith. I want to know Christ and the power of his resurrection and the sharing of his sufferings by becoming like him in his death, if somehow I may attain the resurrection from the dead. Not that I have already obtained this or have already reached the goal; but I press on to make it my own, because Christ Jesus has made me his own. Beloved, I do not consider that I have made it my own; but this one thing I do: forgetting what lies behind and straining forward to what lies ahead, I press on toward the goal for the prize of the heavenly call of God in Christ Jesus.

Zell Kravinsky was a very charitable man. As a Jew, he moved beyond the biblical tithe of 10 percent to even more than 20 percent, more than was recommended by the rabbis in fear that one would leave his family destitute. In time he donated almost all of his money, in fact to worthy causes, most of them in the field of public health. A friend explained his actions: "He gave away the money because he had it and there were people who needed it. But then it began to change the way he looked at himself." Kravinsky read an article in the *Wall Street Journal* and began to investigate the possibility of donating a kidney to someone on a waiting list. His reason, well, there were 60,000 people in the United States currently on the kidney transplant list with only about 15,000 to 20,000 potential donors each year. And only about half of those kidneys would make it to transplant as family members would often refuse to honor even written commitments by their now deceased loved ones. So, Kravinsky decided to make a non-family donation of one of his kidneys to a 29 year old African American woman who was studying for a degree in social work and who had been undergoing dialysis for the last eight years. And Kravinsky felt good about his donation even though some of his friends complained that he made them feel guilty.[54]

Let us pray: May the words of my mouth and the meditations of each of our hearts be acceptable in Your sight, O God, our Rock and our Redeemer. Amen.

Sacrifice is at the heart of our faith. We know that, yet it is also oddly troubling. We think of sacrifice as a worthy activity, but we wonder about the limits of our sacrifice, and we ask things like: Will someone take advantage of my tendency to live a sacrificial lifestyle?

Even so, for the Christian, sacrifice, or risk-taking mission, is primarily a matter of faith. And Paul's words to the Philippians can be helpful as we wrestle with the meaning of risk-taking Mission. He writes: *"I regard everything as loss* I am willing to sacrifice everything *because of the surpassing value of knowing Christ Jesus, my Lord."*[55]

Even though we know the value and importance of growing in our family relationships and other friendships, if we are also striving to grow in faith, then the offering of our time, our talents, and our possessions will, like Paul's, take on a sacrificial character. And it's a good thing too, because the church accomplishes its mission in the world through the sacrifices of individuals, through those who do things like: teaching, praying, singing, visiting, giving money, inviting friends, taking prophetic stances, leading worship, reaching beyond their comfort zones, and offering hospitality.

Risk-taking mission and service always involves sacrifice. But, if something is important to us, we will choose to make those sacrifices, right? This is true in our families. This is true in our workplaces. And, it is true in our service to God. And we serve God, or should serve God, with the understanding that a sacrificial life flows out of our experience of grace. We become willing to give of our time, money and energy because of the grace that we have received already from God.

St. Francis prayed it well: "It is in giving that we receive." A vital church is always an adventure of risk-taking mission mixed in with God's grace. It is a journey into weakness that is also a pilgrimage into the grace of God, who strengthens us and calls us forward or as Paul stated: *This one thing I do. Forgetting what lies behind and straining forward to what lies ahead, I press on toward the goal for the prize of the heavenly call of God in Christ Jesus, my Lord.*[56]

What we need to re-discover, I think though, is that risk-taking mission is not stoic, it's not to be seen as "a cross that we must bear," but, instead, it should be seen as a joyous opportunity to elevate or lift our lives, our relationships, and our resources up to God. And when we truly enter into this kind of risky business, our offerings will take on a sacramental symbolism that will reflect the character of our Lord. For it is as we take risks that we are most like God, we are most like our Trinitarian God whose Son was led by the Spirit to be a sacrifice for us. In risk-taking mission we are most like God.

One pastor spoke of his experience at a conference several years ago. He said: One November several years ago, I was attending a conference in downtown Atlanta, Georgia. It was late in the afternoon on Sunday. I had bowed out of a couple of sessions to finish some work in my hotel room. Time slipped away from me and when I finally went out to find a place to eat, I found that the only place open was a fast food restaurant. As I prepared to enter the restaurant, a young man who was obviously homeless approached me and asked if I would give him money for something to eat. A police officer stepped in to keep him from bothering me. I told the officer that I very much appreciated him doing his job, but that it was okay; I would talk to the young man. Instead of giving him money, I offered to buy him dinner. So we took our place in line, and when we reached the counter, we both ordered our meals. As we left the counter with our respective trays in hand, he looked somewhat watchful, seeing where I was going to sit, and then started to walk away to sit somewhere else. I invited him to join me, and with a look of surprise on his face, he accepted. I must say, in one sense, it was very difficult to enjoy my meal. As a homeless man, he had not bathed in quite a while. But in another sense, it was one of the most profound moments of my life that completely changed my perspective on risk-taking mission and service. After we had finished eating and were preparing to leave, he thanked me and said: "You know, everyone who buys me dinner takes their food and sits somewhere else, leaving me to sit by myself.

But you sat with me and talked to me and spent time with me. I often feel lonely, thank you for your time."[57] The most important thing to this young man was not that a kind person filled his stomach for a few hours, but that he was willing to give a few moments of his time, talking with him. And when the young man pointed that out to his new found friend, that which was just moments ago uncomfortable, to say the least, became an offering which rose up to God and changed both of their lives for the better. But here's the sad thing, too often the church replaces risk-taking mission with charity, that of giving from a distance.

Now, don't misunderstand, charity is an important thing that we do as a church, but is it sufficient? Is it enough? And can such giving evolve into a replacement for the risk-taking mission that is so important to God? Instead of only providing for those who are hungry or in need of shelter or basic human needs, what if we made it a point to join them for dinner? What if we, not only, offered them a cup of soup in Jesus' name but also gave Jesus Himself to them through our presence as we shared a meal with them? What if we not only invited them to worship but also brought them to worship and sat with them? Those in need will indeed take what we offer them. If we offer them a hot meal they will take it. The question we must ask ourselves, as followers of Jesus, who actually spent time with those on the fringes, is this: Will they take more? Will they accept our time and presence and our friendship? And, are we willing to give a part of our lives as we strive to offer Jesus, to others, through our presence with them?

The truth of the matter is that charity that of giving from a distance, many times, is what we do for ourselves, well because it makes us feel better. But on the other hand, risk-taking mission and service is what we do for others because we know that we, the church, exist for them. Risk-taking mission and service is all about being in relationship with those whom Jesus wants to be in relationship with, up close and personal, as personal as sharing a meal or a place in our pew.

But, such mission and service is risky. Because, it forces us to be vulnerable, it challenges us to step out of our comfort zone. We do it though, because we know that the lives of those who Jesus loves depend on it, as well as our own personal growth in Christ.

And, here's the wonderful part. When we the church are willing to step out and take a risk, we will discover a kind of joy and satisfaction that far surpasses the momentary thrill of charitable giving. Why? Well, because we will have discovered the adventure that is the gospel, we will have become a part of the gospel as we allow the good news of Christ to flow through us. And that folks is what we are here for.

Let us pray: Gracious God, we have good intentions. We truly want to help those in need. We desire for all people to come to Christ. We confess that there are times when we have used charity as a replacement for the risk-taking mission and service You have called us to do.

We know that we cannot step out in such mission and service without the presence and power of Your Holy Spirit in our lives. So in the power of Your Spirit, we ask that You assist us as we move forward in our task, knowing that we, Your church, exist not for ourselves, but for others. We lift our prayer to You, Lord God, in the name of Your Son, Jesus Christ, who is the biggest Risk-taker of all. Amen.

A Faithful Way of Living

2 Corinthians 8:1-15

We want you to know, brothers and sisters, about the grace of God that has been granted to the churches of Macedonia; for during a severe ordeal of affliction, their abundant joy and their extreme poverty have overflowed in a wealth of generosity on their part. For, as I can testify, they voluntarily gave according to their means, and even beyond their means, begging us earnestly for the privilege of sharing in this ministry to the saints-- and this, not merely as we expected; they gave themselves first to the Lord and, by the will of God, to us, so that we might urge Titus that, as he had already made a beginning, so he should also complete this generous undertaking among you. Now as you excel in everything--in faith, in speech, in knowledge, in utmost eagerness, and in our love for you --so we want you to excel also in this generous undertaking. I do not say this as a command, but I am testing the genuineness of your love against the earnestness of others. For you know the generous act of our Lord Jesus Christ, that though he was rich, yet for your sakes he became poor, so that by his poverty you might become rich. And in this matter I am giving my advice: it is appropriate for you who began last year not only to do something but even to desire to do something-- now finish doing it, so that your eagerness may be matched by completing it according to your means. For if the eagerness is there, the gift is acceptable according to what one has--not according to what one does not have. I do not mean that there should be relief for others and pressure on you, but it is a question of a fair balance between your present abundance and their need, so that their abundance may be for your need, in order that there may be a fair balance. As it is written, "The one who had much did not have too much, and the one who had little did not have too little."

As we have worked through the Five Practices of Fruitful Congregations: Radical Hospitality, Passionate Worship, Intentional faith development, risk-taking mission and now Extravagant generosity, I have come to see how they are all wrapped up together. I've also come to understand what it means to give in a different way. Extravagant generosity is not about our money. No, instead it is about our hearts. It's not about the support of this church; it's about doing the kingdom-building work of Jesus Christ. Money is a factor, but extravagant generosity involves much more than that.

Let us pray: May the words of my mouth and the meditations of each of our hearts be acceptable in Your sight, O God, our Rock and our Redeemer. Amen.

In our scripture reading for today, the apostle Paul is writing to the people in Corinth and he's talking about money. But listen carefully to his words, Paul writes: *We want you to know, brothers and sisters, about the grace of God that has been granted to the churches of Macedonia; for during a severe ordeal of affliction, their abundant joy and their extreme poverty have overflowed in a wealth of generosity on their part. For, as I can testify, they voluntarily gave according to their means, and even beyond their means, begging us earnestly for the privilege of sharing in this ministry to the saints -- and this, not merely as we expected; they gave themselves first to the Lord and then by the will of God, to us.*[58]

Extravagant generosity is a generous giving of our very selves. Jesus' answer to the question: "How should I live?" was "Love God and your neighbor." Here's a great story. It's about loving others. There was once a little boy in a war-torn, devastated town in Europe during WW II.

He was a little street urchin who had nothing and there he stood in front of a bakery that somehow survived and was still open. In the window were these beautiful, delicious-looking muffins. And the little boy just stood there staring at them. An American GI drove up in his jeep, got out, and said to the little boy: "Doesn't that look good?" And the little boy responded: "Boy, it sure does, especially when you are as hungry as I am." The GI took him inside and bought a dozen of those muffins for him. And as the soldier handed the muffins to the little boy, the boy looked up into his face and said: "Mister, are you God?" And you know what? At that very moment he was like God, in that he reflected God's love and compassion for a hungry little boy. He was offering the compassion that we all need to have. We need to heed the compassion command to love our neighbor, and in order to do that we have to start by emptying ourselves.

We need to empty ourselves so that we might be filled up. Empty ourselves of whatever it is that stands between us and being the loving person that God is calling us to be. Jesus is our example. In Philippians 2, we hear how Jesus emptied Himself. Though He was God, He didn't think equality with God was something to hold on to. Instead He gave up His divine privileges, took the humble position of a slave, and was born as a human being. When He appeared in human form, he humbled Himself in obedience to God and died a criminal's death on a cross. By doing that, He made room for each of us in the kingdom of God. He became an example for us, in how we should live, and how we should die to self. And when we live like that and die to self, we become more thoughtful, more caring, more compassionate people. We become people who are more loving and, therefore, more lovable. That's the consequence of emptying ourselves so that the Holy Spirit may begin to fill us and make us more like Christ.

After talking about how Jesus emptied Himself, Paul goes on to talk about his own self, saying: *I have learned the secret of being content in any and every situation. I can do everything through Christ who gives me strength. My God will meet all your needs according to His glorious riches in Christ Jesus.*[59] What he is trying to tell us, is that no matter what our circumstances, God will provide for all our needs. And through all the ups and downs, God will be there to strengthen us.

Paul was not defined by his circumstances and we don't have to be either. Here's another story. It is about a man who owned a horse. And one day the man's horse ran away. And his friend said: "So sorry about your horse." The man replied, "Bad news, good news, who knows?" A few days later the horse came back with a herd of wild horses. And the man's friend said: "Wonderful!" The man said: "Good news, bad news, who knows?" The next day one of the wild horses threw the man's son and broke both of his son's legs. "How awful," said the friend. "Bad news, good news, who knows?" the man said. Later all of the village's young men were called into war, but the son with the broken legs was excused. "Good news, bad news, who knows?" the man said.

You know, in Paul's story we hear echoes of this story. He too, refuses to be defined by his circumstances. In fact, he has a kind of indifference, a holy indifference, as he writes to the Philippians, saying: *In any and all circumstances I have learned the secret of being well-fed and of going hungry, of having plenty and of being in need.*[60] Paul knows who he is and he refuses to be defined or overcome by externals. One scholar commented on Paul's disposition, saying: He is able to live in abundance, but it is not necessary that he have it. He is able to live in hunger, but it is not necessary that he be poor. He is defined neither by wealth nor by poverty, but by a contentment that transcends both, and by a power in Christ which enables him to live in any circumstance.[61]

I feel that this is the word of the Lord for us this morning. Because too often we are defined, overcome, overwhelmed, demoralized, impressed, and shaped, by external circumstances. But, equally important, perhaps more important really, is what is going on within us. What happens around us is not as important as what happens within us. Think about this, Paul is in prison as he writes the letter to the Philippians, and yet he refuses to see himself as a victim, instead, he sees himself as a person who is empowered by God in any circumstance. He has a very healthy attitude.

But, when bad things happen to good people, how can we respond, as Paul responded? Well, we can work on our own spiritual lives, we can look within, and we can claim a radical faith in our God who is trustworthy, to provide in all circumstances. Working on our own spiritual lives is essential if we want to step up into a faithful way of living.

What we are talking about today is generosity of self. And in order to be generous with self, we must first empty ourselves of anything that is unhealthy. Many people in Welcoming Congregations across the United Methodist Church are discovering that a good way to empty themselves of unhealthy things in their lives is by participating in recovery ministries within their own congregation. Through this process they are able to empty themselves of the bad and open themselves to God's healing grace. They are able to reach a place where they can give themselves away. And once we reach that same place, we, like them, will experience a fresh infilling of God's Holy Spirit, as we become more and more like Christ. We will be equipped to help and lift the burdens of others in the world around us, serving others by becoming the hands and feet of Christ.

Now, I can give example after example of someone lifting the burden of another in this church. But what I'm talking about means so much more than that. I'm talking about lifting the burdens of people who have never set foot on this property. That's different. What I am talking about requires that we make the decision to go beyond the goals we might set at any given time.

You know, goals are fine. But when we set them, guess what, along comes the Holy Spirit with an inspiration that says: "Why don't you just do a little more. Why don't you go just a little beyond what you thought you could do in the first place?" If we ever reach the goal that God sets for this church, well, then it's time to go on to heaven and to be with our Lord. We should always be stretching ourselves beyond what we believe we can do as the Holy Spirit pulls us and directs us and empowers us to do more than we ever imagined possible.

No goal is too great for our God. God's goals are always out there ahead of us. And when we find ourselves operating with the mind-set that we can always do more, we will become a people who do surprising and wonderful things, things we never thought we could do, or wanted to do, or were even willing to do.

We are here to continue to lift the burdens of others as Jesus lifted them. We are here to get involved in the lives of others. We are here to make sacrifices so that someone else can feel the love of Christ through our actions. That is the spirit we are called to have. And when we have that spirit, amazingly we will see the burdens of our own lives becoming less and less.

Jesus essentially says: *"Take up My yoke because it is easy."* It is easy because Jesus is the One who is carrying the weight. He's the One who is providing the strength for the burdens of life. When we take up the yoke of Christ, when we lift the burdens of others through His strength, whether they be health issues, or a loss, or emotional strain, or anything else, a miracle occurs as we realize that our burdens are lifted, as well.

And with that comes, Joy and Peace and Contentment. If you want your life to overflow with Joy and Peace and Contentment, well, you will have to give it away. And you will have to give it away generously. It all comes down to this, I think: As individuals, we must recognize that our self-worth is not defined by the externals. Our self-worth is not defined by our homes, our toys, our degrees, our perks, our jobs, or even by our achievements. But instead, our self-worth is rooted in the grace of God. And once we know that, we can live less anxiously and with more contentment. Paul reminds us: *Do not worry about anything, but in everything by prayer and supplication with thanksgiving let your requests be made known to God. And the peace of God, which surpasses all understanding, will guard your hearts and your minds in Christ Jesus.*[62] He also says: *"Rejoice always, pray without ceasing, give thanks in all circumstances; for this is the will of God in Christ Jesus for you."*[63] And finally, a last word, I want to thank you for your support in so many ways. I want to thank you for your sacrifices. And I want to thank God for your faith, and especially I want to thank God for our partnership in the gospel of Christ. It is all a gift. Every good thing we have, or any good thing we experience, is a gift. It is all God's Amazing Grace.

So, I say trust that God will provide. Even in these unstable times, trust that God will provide in ways that you just can't know of at this time. Do not be defined by external circumstances. And remember that your self-worth is rooted in God's grace and nothing else. And because of that grace, because of that grace, in all circumstances we can be thankful. And so, when that final Trumpet sounds and we can finally see the big picture, we will have to celebrate, we will have to throw a party, because the results, the glorious results of our decisions to give generously, in this lifetime, will be revealed to us in the next!

Wow! What a glorious future we have ahead of us. Praise God! Amen.

Peace Be With You

<u>John 20:19-31</u>
When it was evening on that day, the first day of the week, and the doors of the house where the disciples had met were locked for fear of the Jews, Jesus came and stood among them and said, "Peace be with you." After he said this, he showed them his hands and his side. Then the disciples rejoiced when they saw the Lord. Jesus said to them again, "Peace be with you. As the Father has sent me, so I send you." When he had said this, he breathed on them and said to them, "Receive the Holy Spirit. If you forgive the sins of any, they are forgiven them; if you retain the sins of any, they are retained." But Thomas (who was called the Twin), one of the twelve, was not with them when Jesus came. So the other disciples told him, "We have seen the Lord." But he said to them, "Unless I see the mark of the nails in his hands, and put my finger in the mark of the nails and my hand in his side, I will not believe." A week later his disciples were again in the house, and Thomas was with them. Although the doors were shut, Jesus came and stood among them and said, "Peace be with you." Then he said to Thomas, "Put your finger here and see my hands. Reach out your hand and put it in my side. Do not doubt but believe." Thomas answered him, "My Lord and my God!" Jesus said to him, "Have you believed because you have seen me? Blessed are those who have not seen and yet have come to believe." Now Jesus did many other signs in the presence of his disciples, which are not written in this book. But these are written so that you may come to believe that Jesus is the Messiah, the Son of God, and that through believing you may have life in his name.

As Jesus' disciples hid in the Upper Room after His crucifixion, they were deeply disturbed. But, then Jesus appeared to them and said: "Peace be with you."

Let us pray: May the words of my mouth and the meditations of each of our hearts be acceptable in Your sight, O God, our Rock and our Redeemer. Amen.

Jesus said to His followers that day in the Upper Room: *"Peace be with you."* That is the first of five things that Jesus did that day. First, He gave them words of encouragement, saying: "Peace be with you."

Words are powerful, especially kind words. Kind and affirming words are powerful because they are a means for showing love and acceptance to someone else. That's what Jesus was doing that day in the Upper Room with His friends. He was encouraging them.

The word, encourage, means "to inspire courage." And we need courage. Most of us have more potential than we will ever develop, and what holds us back is often the lack of courage. Jesus knew that about His followers, so He gave them encouraging words. Second, Jesus did not keep a score pad of all the things the disciples had done wrong. Yes, it is true that they all had failed Him in one way or another. But you see Jesus shows us that to truly love another means not keeping score. Third, Jesus made a request that day. He said: *"As the Father has sent Me, so I send you."*[64] In other words He was requesting that they go out and continue the work He had started during His earthly ministry.

But notice this; Jesus made a request, not a demand. When we make a request of another person, we are affirming their worth and their abilities. Now, that person may choose to respond to our request or to deny it, because love always gives a choice. That's what makes it so meaningful.

To know that the other person loves us enough to respond, communicates that they care about us, respect us, admire us and want to do something to please us. Jesus was there that day in the Upper Room to encourage His followers to forgive them, and to affirm their worth.

Fourth, Jesus gave to His disciples, a Gift that day. He said: *"Receive the Holy Spirit."*[65] Jesus had told His disciples, earlier, that He must go away so that the Holy Spirit could come to indwell in God's people.[66] He said to them: *The Advocate, the Holy Spirit, whom the Father will send in My name, will teach you everything, and remind you of all that I have said to you.*[67] Jesus was there that day in the Upper Room to encourage His followers, to forgive them, to affirm their worth, and to give them the Gift of the indwelling Holy Spirit.

Finally, Jesus gave to His followers the gift of His presence. Anyone who has suffered a great loss knows of the greatness of this gift of presence. Being there when another person needs you speaks louder than any spoken words. Physical presence in the time of crisis is one of the most powerful gifts a person can give to another. Jesus knew about the gift of presence. And so He was not only there that one day in the Upper Room, John tells us that: *"Jesus did many other signs in the presence of His disciples."* In other words He spent quality time with them. He knew that togetherness would be important to them. Not only did He return the next week so that Thomas who was not in the Upper Room the first time, so he could see His hands and His side, but He also went to the seashore while the disciples were fishing. John tells us: *After Jesus had appeared to the disciples He showed Himself again to them by the Sea of Tiberias. Gathered there together were Simon Peter, Thomas called the Twin, Nathanael of Cana in Galilee, the sons of Zebedee, and two others of his disciples.*[68]

It seems that Peter had said to them: *"I am going fishing."* And all the others followed him. And just after daybreak, Jesus went to the place where they were fishing and asked them about their catch. Then He cooked breakfast for them, a meal of fish and bread. And they ate together one more time. John then, closes his Gospel account with these words: *There are also many other things that Jesus did; if every one of them were written down, I suppose that the world itself could not contain the books that would be written.*[69] Jesus spent quality time with His disciples after the Resurrection. He was not only present with them, but He participated in activities they could all enjoy. Jesus said to His disciples in the Upper Room that day: *"Peace be with you."* And then He made sure they had that peace by encouraging them, forgiving them, affirming their worth, giving them the Gift of the indwelling Holy Spirit and, spending quality time with them.

And you know what? Jesus offers that same peace to us. And so we must ask ourselves. Are we experiencing that peace of mind, and how can we continue to find peace in our daily walk with Christ? Well, for many of us, peace will come only when we, like those first disciples, come to grips with our past. Many of us, like them, are haunted by the guilt of past failures.

In David Spangler's book, Everyday Miracles, he uses a wonderful analogy to describe the effects of guilt. He writes about one of his favorite places, a swamp in Louisiana that is filled with alligators. You see, this particular swamp had raised sidewalks running alongside the bayou and Spangler had been told that alligators liked marshmallows. He also found out that when he tossed a marshmallow out into the bayou, he could sit back and watch a spectacular show. In a matter of minutes, a pair of eyes would surface and silently glide through the water toward the white, bobbing morsel of sugar. Almost magically, two eyes would become four and four eyes would become six, then eight. He would watch the bushes growing over the water's edge as invariably, alligators would slink out of the shade and paddle over to the marshmallow.

Often without warning, one of the brave reptiles would lunge forward and steal the marshmallow with a quick, powerful snap of its jaws. What was mysterious to Spangler and really creepy, though was the fact that these alligators had silently been watching him all along. No doubt, they and countless others had watched him hike for the mile or so through the swamp and along the bayou. Their piercing eyes and acute sense of smell had sensed the presence of flesh and blood and they had stalked him like any other prey. All the while, he was completely unaware of their hungry vigil. And it wasn't until he tossed the marshmallow out into the water that they revealed their presence: "Those alligators," Spangler said, "are like our memories. Even when we think we are alone and totally free, powerful memories swim just beneath the murky waters of our awareness. Just behind the bushes that grow in the landscapes of our lives are many unsuspected eyes that watch us and, if we allow, control us."[70] What a powerful statement that is. The fact of the matter is, some of us need to come to grips with the alligators in our past.

But, how does a person do that, how do we let go of the past? Well, by realizing that Christ has taken away our past with His death on the cross. Our past failures are gone, forever. Jesus says to His disciples: *"Peace be with you."* And then He shows them His hands and His side. He shows them the marks of the cross, the marks that finalize God's promise made way back in the Garden with Adam and Eve, when God said that one day the "Seed" of Eve, Christ, would *"crush the head of the serpent."*[71] And with the crushing of the serpent's head, would come the canceling of sin. Because of Christ's sacrifice, our past has been washed away, much like the clearing of an Etch-a-Sketch. Because of Christ, it is like our sins have never happened. A person receives the full benefit of the Cross, and experiences the Peace of Christ, when they come to grips with their past, by realizing that Jesus Christ has wiped the slate clean.

But, then there is the future. Others will need to come to grips with the future. Some are living troubled lives because they are terrified of what tomorrow may bring. But, in the book of Hebrews we hear these encouraging words: *"God said, 'I will never leave you, nor forsake you.'"*[72]

You know, it's interesting to find out that in the Greek: "Never" is really a compounding of five negatives. Not that each negative is added to another, but rather that each negative is multiplied by the other. And the word "Leave" means, "to leave behind, to abandon, to give up on, or to send back." And "forsake" means, "to leave one in a helpless state," "to disregard," or to "relax ones watchfulness over another." So actually the verse, in its full, amplified version should read something like this: *God said: I will never, no not ever, no never give up on you, abandon you, leave you behind, cause you not to survive, leave you helpless, nor shall I ever relax when it comes to watching over you.* In other words, because God doesn't relax, we can. God will always be there for us. The good news is that God will not ever abandon us.

How does a person find peace of mind? First, by coming to grips with the past, and then letting go of it. It's gone. The Lord has forgiven you. And second, by not worrying about the future. After all, that's what the whole Easter event is all about. The same God who raised Christ from the dead, watches over you, always, from this day and throughout eternity. *"Peace be with you,"* Jesus says.

I trust you will take His words seriously, and will receive His forgiveness fully, so that you can leave with the Peace that Christ wants for you this day. Peace be with you, the Lord says. Peace be with you. Amen.

Resurrection Reality

Luke 24:36b-48

...Jesus himself stood among them and said to them, "Peace be with you." They were startled and terrified, and thought that they were seeing a ghost. He said to them, "Why are you frightened, and why do doubts arise in your hearts? Look at my hands and my feet; see that it is I myself. Touch me and see; for a ghost does not have flesh and bones as you see that I have." And when he had said this, he showed them his hands and his feet. While in their joy they were disbelieving and still wondering, he said to them, "Have you anything here to eat?" They gave him a piece of broiled fish, and he took it and ate in their presence. Then he said to them, "These are my words that I spoke to you while I was still with you--that everything written about me in the law of Moses, the prophets, and the psalms must be fulfilled." Then he opened their minds to understand the scriptures, and he said to them, "Thus it is written, that the Messiah is to suffer and to rise from the dead on the third day, and that repentance and forgiveness of sins is to be proclaimed in his name to all nations, beginning from Jerusalem. You are witnesses of these things.

One day a 4th grade teacher asked the kids in her class to name who they considered to, be the greatest human being alive in the world today, and the responses were colorful and quite varied. One little boy spoke up and said: "I think it's Tiger Woods. He's the greatest golfer in the world, ever." A little girl said: "I think it's the Pope because he cares for people." And yet another little boy said: "I think it's my mom because she takes care of me and my brother." Over and over again, kids cited one celebrity after another. But then it was little Donnie's turn.

And without even hesitating, when the teacher asked him the question, he replied: "Well I think it's Jesus Christ because He loves everybody and is always ready to help them." Ms. Thompson smiled and said: "Well I certainly like your answer Donnie, because, I also admire Jesus. But there's one slight thing that's wrong. I said the greatest living person, and of course Jesus lived and died almost two thousand years ago. Do you have another name in mind?" And with the simple innocence of a child, little Donnie responded: "Oh no, Ms. Thompson, that's not right at all. Jesus Christ is alive. He lives in me right now!"[73] The greatest affirmation of the Church, in my opinion, is not the affirmation that Jesus performed incredible miracles, or that He was a profound teacher, or even that He showed us what God is like. But, instead it's the affirmation that Jesus Christ is alive and that He actually lives in the hearts of each and every Christian, even to this day.

Let us pray: May the words of my mouth and the meditations of each of our hearts be acceptable in Your sight, O God, our Rock and our Redeemer. Amen.

Our passage this morning from Luke 24 is preceded with the wonderful story of two disciples on the road to Emmaus. This story was told, remembered and cherished by the Christian community because it helped them to appropriate Easter into their lives. The question emerging from the Emmaus story is not the question: "How did God raise Jesus from the dead," or even "Why did God raise Jesus from the dead?" No, it's much more personal, it's more like: "How does Easter get into us?"

Easter in us, the divine presence among us, that is what is important. In this story, the Resurrection becomes as personal and intimate as the sharing of a family meal. Likewise, in our lives, we like the two on the road to Emmaus, must learn to move from the pre-Easter Jesus to the post-Easter Jesus.

Jesus ascended into heaven 40 days after He was resurrected. Even so, His followers continued to experience His presence, but in a radically new way. They no longer experienced Him as a figure of flesh and blood, but as a spiritual reality. They no longer experienced Him as limited by time and space, but as one who could be experienced anywhere, anytime. This experience has continued through the centuries. And it ranges from a dramatic encounter with the Lord like that of the apostle Paul's, to a quieter sense of His presence with us. Jesus is not a figure from the past, but of the present.

The Resurrection is an amazing thing. In fact, let me suggest that our scripture reading today, points to at least three amazing things about the Resurrection: The Reality of it, the Reason for it and the Reach of it.

First, the mere reality of the Resurrection is amazing. We are told that when Jesus walked into the room where the disciples had gathered and said: *"Peace be with you,"* it startled them. They were frightened. It's a ghost, they thought. What else could it be? They were not the kind of people who were easily convinced. They were common sense people and so they doubted. And this doubting, well if you think about it, makes the Resurrection that much more believable. It's a plain story; it's a simple story. It gets right to the point and it's realistic. It's not a manufactured story. It doesn't try to prove anything.

Look at some of the other parts of the story. First they are startled and frightened. Then Jesus tries to calm them down. Then He invites them to touch Him. Now, you can put your hand through a ghost but evidently, you can't put your hand through a glorified body. They examine the scars on His feet and hands. But, it seems that they still don't believe. So He tries something different. *"Do you have anything here to eat,"* He asks. Which raises another question: Can a ghost eat food? They give Him a piece of broiled fish and He eats in their presence.

Finally He sits down with them and begins to teach them about why everything happened as it did. It was to fulfill the Old Testament prophecies. That's simple isn't it? It was God's will that things happened as they did. The Resurrection is a reality. It's an impossible thing that happened. And maybe it's the simplicity of it that convinces us.

Secondly, the reason for the Resurrection is amazing. The reason it happened, was for the forgiveness of sins. That's what Jesus told His disciples. It happened so you and I and everyone else we know might have a new start with life. It happened so we might have the chance to start over, and continue on with God.

Let me tell you a true story that happened some years ago to a friend and colleague of mine: A young boy's father died in a car wreck when he was twelve years old. And he read the news in the paper before anyone was able to tell him about it. When he saw the picture of the family car smashed-up on the front page of the newspaper, and read that his dad had died in that accident, he was thrust immediately into numbness and grief. Strangely, one of his very first feelings was that of guilt. He had remembered how a few months before at a family picnic he was showing off with a baseball. At one point he got careless and threw it wildly. It hit his dad in the hand and broke his thumb. The young boy felt horrible. He said to himself: "What a terrible son I am. I have caused my dad great pain." It seemed that all he could remember after his father's death was the pain he caused his dad. Finally, the young boy went to see his pastor and told him about the deep feelings of guilt and about breaking his dad's thumb. And upon later reflection, he said: I'll never forget how my pastor handled that. He was so great. He came around the desk with tears in his eyes. He sat down across from me and said: "Now, Jim, you listen to me. If your dad could come back to life for five minutes and be right here with us, and if he knew you were worried about that, what would he say to you?"

"He would tell me to quit worrying about that," Jim said. "Well, all right," the minister said, "then you quit worrying about that right now. Do you understand me?" "Yes sir," Jim said, and he did.[74]

That minister was saying: You are forgiven. Accept the forgiveness, and make a new start with your life. The young boy did make a new start. And he became the pastor of a 7,000 membership church in Houston. The young boy was Reverend James W. Moore.

On Easter, the Risen Lord comes back to life, and assures the disciples that they are forgiven. Peter had denied his Lord three times. Thomas had doubted. All the disciples had forsaken Him. But, Christ came back, forgave them and offered them New Life. He came back to share with them, just as He comes today, this morning, to share with you the joy, the encouragement and the forgiveness of Easter. The reason for the Resurrection, forgiveness of sins is an amazing thing. And it sounds impossible, but it happened for that reason.

And finally, the reach of the resurrection is amazing. This message of forgiveness is to be carried everywhere we go. Repentance and forgiveness of sins, said Jesus, will be preached in His name to all nations, beginning at Jerusalem. Notice He said beginning at Jerusalem. It is not to be confined within the walls of any city, any home, or any church. We cannot expect the world to come to Jerusalem to hear the message. Jerusalem must go to the world. Jesus did not command the whole world to go to the church. He commanded His church to go to the whole world.

When Jesus explained to the disciples the reason for the Resurrection He immediately told them and us to reach the world with that message. And Jesus gives the Power to do so.

The disciples were told to stay in the city and wait until the Power of the Lord came upon them. And when it did on the day of Pentecost, they became like people filled by the Holy Spirit as they witnessed about the life, death and Resurrection of their Lord. Likewise, we, too, must be open to that Power from on high, constantly petitioning God to fill us with His Holy Spirit. Then we will be ready to assist Him, as we witness for Christ in this world. He gives us the power to do that. It's ours.

It's amazing isn't it, that the story of the Resurrection is now in your hands and my hands. It's ours to use, to reach out with, to pass on to our children and to our neighbors. Don't keep it. Don't confine it to the walls of Jerusalem. The Resurrection of Jesus is a message to the nations, an amazing, joyful, impossible story that happened. It's a simple story; that's what makes it so real. It is a story of forgiveness; that's why we need to talk about it. It is a story for all nations; that's how far we are to take it.

Jesus gives the Power to take His story to the nations. He places that wonderfully, exciting task in our hands. It's our job now, to tell the whole world about the reality of His Resurrection. It's our turn to tell the world about what the acceptance of that reality really means. So, beginning this very day, I challenge you to pray for that Power from on high. And then ask God to open your eyes to how you might best share His story of forgiveness right here in Chappell Hill. Amen.

A Book Like No Other

Nehemiah 8:1-3, 5-6, 8-12

All the people gathered together into the square before the Water Gate. They told the scribe Ezra to bring the book of the law of Moses, which the LORD had given to Israel. Accordingly, the priest Ezra brought the law before the assembly, both men and women and all who could hear with understanding. This was on the first day of the seventh month. He read from it facing the square before the Water Gate from early morning until midday, in the presence of the men and the women and those who could understand; and the ears of all the people were attentive to the book of the law. And Ezra opened the book in the sight of all the people, for he was standing above all the people; and when he opened it, all the people stood up. Then Ezra blessed the LORD, the great God, and all the people answered, "Amen, Amen," lifting up their hands. Then they bowed their heads and worshiped the LORD with their faces to the ground. So they read from the book, from the law of God, with interpretation. They gave the sense, so that the people understood the reading. And Nehemiah, who was the governor, and Ezra the priest and scribe, and the Levites who taught the people said to all the people, "This day is holy to the LORD your God; do not mourn or weep." For all the people wept when they heard the words of the law. Then he said to them, "Go your way, eat the fat and drink sweet wine and send portions of them to those for whom nothing is prepared, for this day is holy to our LORD; and do not be grieved, for the joy of the LORD is your strength." So the Levites stilled all the people, saying, "Be quiet, for this day is holy; do not be grieved." And all the people went their way to eat and drink and to send portions and to make great rejoicing, because they had understood the words that were declared to them.

Today, I would like to share with you several reasons I think that the Bible cannot be matched by any other. It connects us to the power of God. It provides comfort when life is challenging. It reveals the Truth; it gives insight and guidance for living life to the fullest. And finally, it shows us the way to salvation.

Let us pray: May the words of my mouth and the meditations of each of our hearts be acceptable in Your sight, O God, our Rock and our Redeemer. Amen.

There was once a professor who was in a terrible accident that left him in a body cast for six months. The doctors were concerned that he would not be able to walk normally ever again. And it was during that time that a story from the Bible connected this professor to the healing power of God, the story was the one about the paralytic who was brought to Jesus for healing. The professor began to recall that story during physical therapy in the hospital while taking his first steps between parallel bars: "two steps the first day, four the next," he said. But the most frequent recollections of the story were during the months of his physical therapy at home. He told himself that story time after time. Sometimes it was a story of hope where he would envision himself walking again. Often it was a story of forgiveness; forgiveness for his sins of avoiding or not doing his exercises. And it was also a story which gave him a context for exploring his own skepticism, about God's ability to heal him. He said: "In the process of remembering the story, Jesus Christ became present for me. The return of my strength and energy was a steady gift that was profoundly connected to the story, and somehow, God used it to enable me to walk again."[75] Now, there's a man who would agree that no other text, no science book, no theology book, no collection of poems, or any other book could have connected him to the power of God like the Bible did. First, the Bible connects us to the power of God and second, it provides comfort when life is challenging.

There was once a pastor (Martin Niemoeller) who opposed Hitler during World War II and so, he spent much of the war in a German prison camp. They took from him everything except his Bible. After his release, the pastor gave this testimony, saying: What did the Bible mean to me during the long and weary years of solitary confinement? Well, the word of God was simply everything to me, comfort and strength, guidance and hope, master of my days and companion of my nights, the bread that kept me from starvation and the Living Water that refreshed my soul.

And then there was a well-known theologian (Juergen Moltmann) who shared how he became a Biblical scholar. He wrote: "I was drawn into the reading of the Bible when I got my first copy from an American Army chaplain as a young prisoner of war (in Belgian) in 1945. The book of Lamentation spoke to me when I felt completely lost and forsaken. And the Passion story of Jesus touched my soul because I felt that Christ understood me and my situation. Step after step I discovered the Gospel and the promise of God for the poor and the imprisoned. The Bible was the book that rescued me from resignation and despair," he said.

Did you hear that? Here we have testimony from two people who witnessed to the fact, that even though circumstances could imprison their physical body, they could not imprison their soul. Why? Well, because they were able to feel God's presence with them, through His written Word. They could be put in chains and shackles but, because of the Word of God, their dreams and hopes remained intact.

It has been said that other books have been written for our information, but the Bible was given for our transformation. That's exactly what happens when we read it and allow its message to live within us. First, the Bible connects us with the power of God. Second, it provides comfort when we need it most and third, it confirms God's Truth and gives insight for life.

In 2 Timothy 3:16 we hear that *"all scripture is inspired by God, and profitable for teaching and instruction."* And in Psalm 119:105 we are taught: *"Thy word (God's Word) is a lamp unto our feet and a light unto our path."* You know, the primary purpose of the Church is to study God's word and then apply its eternal truth to whatever situation may present its self to us even in our present day.

W.H. Auden once declared: "The Bible is the News that is always new." John Wesley, the founder of Methodism, said: "We are to be a people of one Book. This one Book is to judge all the other books that we read for their accuracy and their trustworthiness." And, it was the great reformer, Martin Luther, who developed what we call the Great Protestant Principle: "Sola scriptura," which means, it is by scripture alone that we discover and learn the ultimate will of God. But one of the biggest problems we have these days, I think, is that we set God's Word aside when we have decisions to make. In fact we turn it all around sometimes, by making up our minds first, and then trying to find some biblical text to support what we have already decided.

But, that's the opposite of what the apostle Paul teaches. He teaches that we should read God's word, first, get convicted, and then make our decisions line up with God's plan. In order for that to happen, though, our conscience must be re-programmed. And only God's word through the work of His Holy Spirit can do that. In the Book of 2 Chronicles, there is a story about a priest who was cleaning the Temple where he discovered in the corner a book. It was called the Book of Law, or the Book of Life. The nation he loved was in great turmoil, morality was non-existent and the nation had forgotten its heritage and roots. The discovery of the book in the Temple, and the people's new-found allegiance to it, restored the nation to true greatness in the eyes of God. And in our reading for today from Nehemiah it is that same Book that Ezra the scribe, reads to the people who had just rebuilt the walls around Jerusalem. And not only was the Word of God read to them, but the people stood, possibly for hours, and listened intently.

Why? Well, because they knew that the words found in that book were inspired by God. They knew that they were somehow Living words, and that God would use His word to show them the way to abundant life.

Do you think God still does that today? I do. Many times He brings back into our memory words of scripture, assuring words, comforting words, words that bring peace, supporting words, whatever it is that we might need at any given moment. You know, it's amazing, God knows what we need much better than we know ourselves. And so it only makes sense that we should always be in God's Word, searching the scriptures for guidance from the One who knows us best. And it only makes sense that we should always strive to take God's word to heart, every single day, doesn't it?

First, the Bible connects us with the power of God. Second, it provides comfort when we need it most and third, it confirms God's Truth and gives insight for life. And finally, the Bible shows us the way to Salvation. God offers to all who will receive, a precious gift of salvation, abundant life now and Eternal life, well, forever. That's what eternal means, right? Praise God for His Power, Comfort, Truth and Wisdom. Praise God for His presence with us, for His willingness to enter into our lives and into this world. Praise God for His forgiveness, His grace and His mercy. Praise God!

Have you ever heard the children's song: "The B- I-B-L-E?" It goes like this: The B-I-B-L-E now that's the book for me. I stand alone on the Word of God, the B-I-B-L-E.

Let's sing it together; I love that song, and I think John Wesley would have liked it too. He once said: "I want to know one thing, the way to salvation. God Himself has condescended, has stooped down to teach the way. He has written it down in a Book. O, give me that Book! At any price, give me that Book of God!"

John Wesley was a man of one Book. He believed that everything needed to find the way to salvation was contained within the Holy Scriptures. And so, my challenge to you today is to pick up the Book that Wesley held in such high esteem. Read it and decide for yourself. Who knows maybe you, too will say: "O give me that Book! At any price, give me the Book of God. For, now I too, am a person of one Book." So be it. Amen.

Led By The Spirit

Romans 8:12-17

So then, brothers and sisters, we are debtors, not to the flesh, to live according to the flesh-- for if you live according to the flesh, you will die; but if by the Spirit you put to death the deeds of the body, you will live. For all who are led by the Spirit of God are children of God. For you did not receive a spirit of slavery to fall back into fear, but you have received a spirit of adoption. When we cry, "Abba! Father!" it is that very Spirit bearing witness with our spirit that we are children of God, and if children, then heirs, heirs of God and joint heirs with Christ--if, in fact, we suffer with him so that we may also be glorified with him.

A young businessman was rushed to a hospital in serious condition. A doctor predicted that he might die. Not a religious man at the time, he did, however, turn on a Christian radio station and heard a song being played: "God Will Take Care of You." He said that he couldn't get that song out of his mind. He began to pray, and as he did, he reported a sense of energy flowing in. It was a Sunday morning and he heard a group of nurses having a brief worship service in a nearby room and so he struggled up out of bed to join them. While there, he committed his life to Jesus Christ. That man recovered. And for the rest of his life, he remained faithful to his commitment. He referred every business and personal decision to God. He was resolute in his ethics and he lived by the teachings of Jesus.[76] You've heard of this man. His name was J. C. Penney. And he insisted throughout his lifetime that God fulfills His promise to give divine help to all who choose to be led by the Spirit.

Let us pray: May the words of my mouth and the meditations of each of our hearts be acceptable in Your sight, O God, our Rock and our Redeemer. Amen.

The Apostle Paul wrote: *All who are led by the Spirit of God are children of God, and have received a spirit of adoption.*[77] Today is a special day, because we have witnessed this morning the Baptism of one of our own, and have welcomed him into the family of Christ. He made a choice for Christ a few weeks ago, and came here today to seal that decision by being baptized in the name of the Father and of the Son and of the Holy Spirit. And even though we are only baptize once in the United Methodist church, because we feel that God gets it right the first time, re-affirmation of faith is a little different. That's what the rest of us did today we re-affirmed our faith, something we do during every baptism. Re-affirmation of faith is a repeatable rite of the church and, I think, that it's a necessary part of our daily walk with God. It's a continuing process. We have to decide everyday if we are going to be led by the Spirit or not.

You know, it's easy to turn away from God's Spirit and to allow something else to lead us. Note how many times, even in our beloved denomination, church members have turned away from God's call, the times they have blocked Him off the calendar thinking "this weekend God won't notice if I'm not in church." And so they slip away into a few more hours of Sunday morning sleep, or into the backyard, or piously putter around the house under the guise of getting caught up, or maybe they pour up a nice cool glass of raspberry tea, and sit out on the front porch. Yes, even church members can be misled by the enticing call of things that would distract them from the fellowship of worship, and it was the same in Paul's day. He warned the people, saying: What are you doing? *You did not receive a spirit of slavery to fall back into fear.*[78]

The people in the Roman church were trying to return to what had previously enslaved them and that was a crippling thing for them. Likewise, some of us are crippled by the mistakes of our past. We lie awake at night re-living past humiliations, anticipating the consequences of past misdeeds, or regretting the tragedy of missed opportunities. But, no teaching is more, clear in Scripture than this. The past is gone. *"Though your sins be as scarlet, they shall be as white as snow,"*[79] the Prophet Isaiah wrote. And Paul advises us in Philippians 3:13 to *"forget those things that are past."*

That's great advice because guilt plays a large role in many people's anxiety. Forget those things that are past, Jesus said. We are also to forget those things that are yet to come. Jesus said in His Sermon on the Mount: *"Do not be anxious about tomorrow... each day has trouble enough of its own."* Concentrate on today. Who knows what tomorrow may bring? Today is the only day we can be certain of.

Norman Vincent Peale had a marvelous illustration. He told a story about when he and his wife once drove up to their summer place after dark. A rough path of stepping stones led from the parking area to the house, he said. And on stepping out of the car with a flashlight, he discovered that it would not illuminate the entire path, just the stones directly in front of them. However, he realized that if they would just take one stepping stone at a time, they could reach the house safely.[80] That's how life is best lived, focusing on one day, one step or one task at a time. Focus on today and don't worry about tomorrow or yesterday: *You did not receive a spirit of slavery to fall back into fear, Paul says but you have received a spirit of adoption.*[81]

Now, certainly, there are legitimate things in this world to fear, but God is greater than them all. Forget about the past and the future. Focus on today. Enjoy it to the fullest. Focus on those things you can control, and not on those you can't control.

Do the best you can and entrust the rest to God. Focus on your faith, and not on your fears. Think on God's goodness and His power rather than on your own frailties. Do not be enslaved to your fears any longer, Paul says. Let God help you break those chains. Take ownership of the new spirit of trust and hope and joy and love that God offers to you. Rejoice in your new identity as a son or daughter of God.

Also, just knowing that we are children of God should make us more aware of our brothers and sisters in Christ, too. Paul continues: *Now if we are children, then we are heirs -- heirs of God and co-heirs with Christ, if indeed we share in His sufferings in order that we may also share in His glory.*[82]

How do we share in Christ's sufferings? We do so in love and compassion for our fellow co-heirs. We understand we are very special people, but we also realize that we are followers of the humble Galilean. And we live our lives as He would live His life.

What I want to emphasize this morning is that there is hope, hope for all, if only we turn to Christ and rely on His Spirit daily, trusting that God is here, at work in our lives to transform us. But, before such real transformation can come about, I think, that we have to understand why change is necessary.

The Bible provides a fascinating assessment of the condition of humanity. God's Word asserts that every human being is a slave to desire. Every person is born with a particular set of desires, desires that could lead us away from God and into lives of frustration. If we choose to turn our life and will over to Christ, however, we are given a brand new set of desires, desires that will lead us to please God and ultimately to fulfillment in our own being. The important thing to note, though, is that our slavery to desire is not negotiable. The only choice we have is which desire we will obey.

Does this mean that we aren't free? Does this mean that we are not at liberty to choose whatever we want to do at a given moment? Well, the fact of the matter is that our choices are almost always determined by our desires. Normally we do what we truly desire at any given moment. As an example, think about this: There is abundant evidence that quality of life is enhanced when we engage in a regular exercise program. And, few people are likely to say: "Being out of shape has been a major asset in my life, and I hope to prolong my time on the couch." No, instead, investments in exercise equipment, workout plans, personal trainers, and specialized clothing have skyrocketed within the last quarter century. A majority of those polled on January 1 indicate that their resolution is to pursue a more vigorous regimen of exercise. However, take a look at our nation. More than 50 percent of Americans are overweight, and 25 percent are technically obese. What has happened to the expressed and even fervent desire for physical conditioning? Well, it is routinely overwhelmed by a greater desire, the desire to eat whatever happens to taste good, and to not "sweat" when it's time to work out. Day by day we obey our greatest desires. And it seems that our resolutions to be in better shape stand little chance as we continually hang out at the local buffets. But, it is through the Second Person of the Trinity, the Holy Spirit that God pours out grace in the midst of our dilemma. Jesus alone delivers the power to change.

Here's something else to think about. Have you ever been riding in an airplane and suddenly started wondering: "How in the world is this thing staying up in the air?" And then we realize the plane is a lot heavier than the air. You know, they can't float. They are not boats in the water; they are planes in the air. And the law of gravity tells us that if something is heavier than air and it is in the air that it must be drawn toward the center of the earth. In fact, for centuries philosophers and inventors concluded that flying is a privilege reserved only for creatures born with wings.

So how is it that right now, as we speak, flights will take off and land all over the world? Well, the answer is Bernoulli's Principle. Airplane wings are curved in such a way that air flows faster above the wing than beneath it. According to Bernoulli's principle, if water or air is flowing faster along one side of an object then that object will be pulled in that direction. That's what gives airplane wings their lift. The law of gravity is not suspended as it may appear. But, airplanes are able to fly simply because they are empowered by a greater law, one that supersedes gravity.[83]

Paul writes: *"The law of the Spirit of life in Christ Jesus has set you free from the law of sin and of death."*[84] In this world God does not suspend our desires. They still reside within us and they remain exceedingly powerful. But Christians can experience victory over those desires because of a higher law, a greater power that supersedes the law of sin. Whenever someone chooses to become an intentional imitator of Jesus Christ, a brand new set of desires is placed in their heart. It's a God thing how this happens. It is done through the power of God's Holy Spirit. Christians receive an entirely new nature. Paul says that Christians are re-created. He says that *"there is a new creation: everything old has passed away, and everything has become new."*[85] And it's because of that new creation that often times, new disciples virtually become intoxicated with excitement about pleasing God. Paul writes: *For you did not receive a spirit of slavery to fall back into fear, but you have received a spirit of adoption. When we cry, 'Abba! Father!' it is that very Spirit bearing witness with our spirit that we are children of God.*[86]

The Holy Spirit whispers to us: "Don't lose heart. You belong to God. You are God's child. You have been rescued by grace and you will never, ever, be rejected." You see, God has already given us the status of righteousness. God looks at Christians right now as His perfect children, because when He looks at us He sees Jesus beside us.

Think about what God has done for you and me. We have been given the ultimate status in the universe; we are God's own children. And all we need to do, to tap into God's power over sin, is to make the decision to be led by God's Spirit daily, rather than by something else.

God's grace is an invitation to grow into the likeness of the One whose name we bear, or as Paul put it: *So then, brothers and sisters, we are debtors, not to the flesh, to live according to the flesh -- for if you live according to the flesh you will die; but if by the Spirit you put to death the misdeeds of the body, you will live.*[87]

Bernoulli's Principle allows airplanes to overcome the law of gravity. But, for a plane to fly, somebody has to start the airplane, taxi it to the runway, and gun the engines to reach sufficient speed to become airborne. Likewise, God provides everything we need to live a spiritual life. But we will never get off the ground unless we make the right decisions and take the right steps to walk with God to be led by His Spirit. What are the right steps? Well, we must decide to follow God by feeding our new desires and starving any old ones that don't line up with God's perfect plan for our lives. Choosing to be Spirit led, is the key to winning the battle. God promises that the Spirit will live inside of us, but we have to make the choice to listen to the Spirit's guidance.

My challenge to you today is to try and listen to the Spirits guidance in everything each and every day. Even when things are not going the way you might wish, I challenge you to take a few seconds, breathe in deeply of the Spirit, listen and then act accordingly, act the way that our gentle Savior would act in that situation. In doing so, not only will you be growing in God's Spirit, but you will, also, be bringing to fruition God's plan, as you continue on your journey with Christ. Amen.

A Step to Freedom

Isaiah 57:18
I have seen their ways, but I will heal them; I will lead them and repay them with comfort, creating for their mourners the fruit of the lips.

There was once a father was trying to take a nap on a Sunday afternoon in his living room and his little boy kept saying: "Daddy, I'm bored." So his father, trying to make up a game, found a picture of a globe in the newspaper, a picture of the world. He ripped it up in about fifty pieces and said: "Son this is a puzzle. I want you to put it all back together." Then he laid down to finish his nap, thinking he would get at least another hour and a half of sleep. But, in about 15 minutes the little boy woke him up saying: "Daddy, I've got it finished. It's all put together." "You're kidding," his father said. "How did you do that?" And the little boy replied: "Well, there was a picture of a person on the back page of that newspaper and when I got my person put together the world looked just fine."

We're beginning a new series today called the "Road to Recovery." It's going to work on our person. And you know what? It is amazing how much better the world looks when our person is put together in the right way.

Let us pray: May the words of my mouth and the meditations of each of our hearts be acceptable in Your sight, O God, our Rock and our Redeemer. Amen.

Today we're going to talk about how to handle, and how to overcome the hurts in our lives, things that may be messing up our lives or have caused us pain. Hurts, habits, and hang-ups, that's what we will call them.

Our scripture reading this morning was very short so let me read it to you again. It comes from the book of Isaiah. God is speaking, He says: *I have seen how they acted but I will heal them, I will lead them and help them and I will comfort those who mourn. I offer peace to all near and far.*[88] In this great promise of God, notice that there are five things God wants to do in our lives: First, if you have been hurt, God says: "I want to heal you." Second, if you're confused: "I want to lead you." Third, if you've feel helpless to change something, God says: "I want to help you change that." Fourth, if you've feel that no one understands your problem, God says: "I want to comfort you." Fifth, if you feel anxious and worried and afraid, God wants to "offer peace to you."

The fact is this, life is tough. We live in an imperfect world. We have been hurt by other people, we sometimes hurt ourselves, and we sometimes hurt other people. The Bible tells us that: *"All have sinned."* That means none of us are perfect. We've all blown it at times. We've all made mistakes. And so consequently, we hurt, and we hurt others. This series on Celebrating Recovery is for everybody. Everyone in this sanctuary needs recovery, well, that is unless you've lived a perfect life. And, the good news is this, regardless of the problem, the steps to recovery are always the same. They are always the same.

The principles for recovery are found in the Bible. I guess we could say that it is the original recovery manual. And these principles are summarized around the word "R-E-C-O-V-E-R-Y." We will take a letter each week and look at eight steps on this wonderful journey.

So let's begin. The "R" in recovery stands for Realize. Realize I'm not God. I admit I am powerless to control my tendency to do wrong things from time to time. Do you ever stay up late when you know you need to sleep? Do you ever eat or drink more than you know your body needs? Do you ever feel you ought to exercise but you don't? Do you ever know the right thing to do, but you don't do it? Do you ever know something is wrong, but you do it anyway? Have you ever known you should be unselfish, but you're selfish instead? Have you ever tried to control somebody or something and found it was uncontrollable? If your answer is yes to any of these questions, well, welcome to the human race. We all need to recover from something.

But, why is that? Well, you see, we all have a sin nature with us. And our sin nature can get us into all kinds of trouble. We do things that aren't good for us. We react the wrong way to people. Proverbs 14 says: *"There is a way that seems right to a person but it ends in death."* You and I will always have this nature with us, this desire to do the wrong thing. We're going to always have it with us until we get to heaven. Even after we become Christian, we still have desires that pull us the wrong way. Paul understood this. In Romans 7:15 he wrote: *I don't understand myself at all, for I really want to do what's right, but I can't. I do what I don't want to do. I do what I hate. I know perfectly well that what I'm doing is wrong, but I can't help myself. It is sin inside me that's stronger than I am, that makes me do those things.*

The first step to recovery is that of understanding the cause of the problem. What's the cause of the problem? Well, the cause is this. We want to play God. We want to decide what's right and what's wrong. We want to call the shots. We want to make our own rules. We want to put ourselves at the center of the universe. That's called playing God.

This is humanity's oldest problem. Adam and Eve had it. God put them in Paradise and they tried to control Paradise. God said: *"You can do anything you want to in this entire Paradise except one thing: Don't eat from this certain tree."* And what did they do? They made a beeline for that tree. Wanting to play God has been the problem from the very start. Adam and Eve wanted to play God, and so do we.

But, how do we play God? Well, first, we try to control our image. We want to control what other people think of us. Second, we try to control other people. We use a lot of tools to manipulate each other. We use guilt to control; we use fear; we use praise. Sometimes we use the silent treatment to control others. We try to control other people. Third, we try to control problems, our problems. We're good at this. We use phrases like: "I can handle it. It's not really a problem." And forth, we try to control our pain. Sometimes we try to control our pain by eating too much or by not eating enough. We try to control our pain by drinking too much, or by smoking, or by taking drugs, or by getting in and out of relationships. There are many, many ways that people try to control their pain. The fact of the matter is that pain comes when we realize, that we are not God, and that we can't control everything, and that's scary. But, actually, it is during those A'ha moments that recovery can begin.

Okay, what are the consequences of trying to play God? Here are four: First, we experience fear. When we try to control everything, we get afraid. Adam said: *"I was afraid, because I was naked and so I hid myself."* Second, we experience frustration. It's frustrating when we try to be the general manager of the universe. Paul realized this, and so he wrote: *It seems to be a fact of life that when I want to do what is right I inevitably do what is wrong. Something else is deep within me. There is a war with my mind that wins the fight and makes me a slave to the sin.* David understood this too, and he wrote: *"My dishonesty made me miserable and filled my days with frustration."*

Frustration is a symptom of a deeper problem that has not been dealt with. There is a root issue that needs to be uncovered. You know that you are not God, but for some reason, you are trying to take His place, and that doesn't work.

Fatigue is a third consequence of trying to play God. It is very tiring, this trying to play God thing. Trying to control everything and pretending you've got it all together. Well, that's denial and it takes a lot of energy. In Psalm 32, David said: *"My strength evaporated like water on a sunny day until I finally admitted all my sins to You and stopped trying to hide them."* If you're in a constant state of fatigue, always worn out, ask yourself this question: What pain am I running from? What problem do I have, that is motivating me to work so hard, that I'm in the constant state of fatigue?

And finally, failure is a consequence of trying to play God, because playing God is one job you're guaranteed to fail at. Proverbs 28:13 says: *"You'll never succeed in life if you try to hide your sins. Confess them. Give them up. Then God will show mercy to you."* You need to be honest and open about your weaknesses and your faults and failures. But the problem is this: We are not always honest with ourselves much less with someone else. Here are a couple of excuses used by people who are not being honest with themselves. They say: Oh, my problem is not that bad. That's called denial. Hey, save yourself some pain, start early. One man said: "Recovery began, for me, when the acid of my pain finally ate through the wall of my denial." Don't wait until the pain is unbearable. You know, pain is God's megaphone to us. Let it motivate you to get help, to face the issue you've been ignoring ten, twenty, maybe thirty years. How's your pain level? It's a warning signal to you. Listen to it.

Here's another excuse people who are not being honest with themselves use. It goes like this. They say: This recovery thing is fine for others, but I don't need it; I'm doing fine on my own. That's called denial too. Unless you've lived a perfect life, then there are some things you need to deal with. You may say to yourself: I can handle my problem; I can take care of it. But, the fact is this, if you could handle it, you would have already done so. If you could have handled that problem, it wouldn't be a problem. You wouldn't still have it today. But you can't, so it's still with you. This denial thing is as old as Adam and Eve, you know. They had a problem. They ran and hid in the bushes. God had made them and God had made the bushes, and they're hiding from God? Now, that's pretty silly.

Sometimes I've asked certain people: Have you told God about your hurt, your habit, or your hang-up? Oh, no, they answer, I wouldn't want God to know about it. But, you can't get fixed till you 'fess up, face your faults, and admit that you are powerless, first to God and then to someone you trust. So, here it is. The first step on the road to recovery is to admit: I am powerless and I'm not God. Doing this means recognizing three important facts of life. First, I am powerless to change my past. Second, I am powerless to control other people. And third, I am powerless to cope with harmful habits, behaviors and actions.

James 4:6 says: *"God opposes the proud but gives grace to the humble."* Grace is the power to change. Grace is the power God gives to you and me to make the changes in our lives that we, deep down want to make, and that God wants to make in us. So, we need God's grace. How do we get it? Well, there is only one way: God gives it to those who are humble.

Let me ask you: What needs changing in your life? What hurt or hang-up or habit have you been trying to ignore? For many of you this step will be the most difficult step. But, I'm glad it's the first step, because when you get past this one, when you get over this bump in the road, when you are able to admit that you just might have a problem, that you just might have a need, that you just might have a hurt, well then at that realization your life will be opened, for God's healing grace to come in. But, it's hard for many of us to admit these things, because it's humbling. It says: "I'm not God and I don't have it all together as much as I'd like everybody to think that I do." But, if you tell that to somebody, guess what? They're not going to be surprised, because they know it. God knows it; you know it; you just need to say it out loud.

So let's practice; let's say these things together, out loud. Repeat after me: I am not God. And, I don't have it all together. Okay, my challenge to you this morning is to make the decision to join us as we journey through these eight Sundays, really put your heart and mind into the messages, so that we can all travel further, down God's Road of Freedom, Health, and Wholeness. That's what God offers to all who will humble themselves, and open their heart to Him, for healing. Amen.[89]

Where To Find Help

Hebrews 11:6-16

And without faith it is impossible to please God, for whoever would approach him must believe that he exists and that he rewards those who seek him. By faith Noah, warned by God about events as yet unseen, respected the warning and built an ark to save his household; by this he condemned the world and became an heir to the righteousness that is in accordance with faith. By faith Abraham obeyed when he was called to set out for a place that he was to receive as an inheritance; and he set out, not knowing where he was going. By faith he stayed for a time in the land he had been promised, as in a foreign land, living in tents, as did Isaac and Jacob, who were heirs with him of the same promise. For he looked forward to the city that has foundations, whose architect and builder is God. By faith he received power of procreation, even though he was too old--and Sarah herself was barren--because he considered him faithful who had promised. Therefore from one person, and this one as good as dead, descendants were born, "as many as the stars of heaven and as the innumerable grains of sand by the seashore." All of these died in faith without having received the promises, but from a distance they saw and greeted them. They confessed that they were strangers and foreigners on the earth, for people who speak in this way make it clear that they are seeking a homeland. If they had been thinking of the land that they had left behind, they would have had opportunity to return. But as it is, they desire a better country, that is, a heavenly one. Therefore God is not ashamed to be called their God; indeed, he has prepared a city for them.

Some of you are unaware that a couple of Sundays ago, when it rained so hard, there was an area that flooded close to Eric's house. And there are rumors that the Banner Press sent a reporter out there where he found Christopher, Eric's son, sitting on the roof as things were floating by. So he climbed up on the roof with Christopher, and the first thing he saw was a chicken coop floating by and then he saw this horse and then he saw this VW bug floating by. Then after a few minutes he saw this hat float by, but after it got about twenty feet past the house the hat started floating back upstream. Then it got about twenty feet on the other side of the house and it started floating back downstream again. He watched this, seven or eight times, and finally he said: "Christopher, do you have any idea what that hat's all about?" And Christopher said: "Oh, that's just my crazy dad, on his tractor. He said he was going to mow the pasture come Hades or high water."[90] You know, the problem we have today is that a lot of us are still focusing on the little things while the house is floating downstream.

Let us pray: May the words of my mouth and the meditations of each of our hearts be acceptable in Your sight, O God, our Rock and our Redeemer. Amen.

Last week we said, all of us need recovery because none of us is perfect. But it is easy to be in denial about that, it is easy to ignore that our house is floating downstream, while focusing on other things in life. But the fact of the matter is this, the world is imperfect. We are imperfect, we've all been hurt, we all have hang-ups; we all have habits we'd like to change. Everyone has something God wants to work on.

Last Sunday, we talked about the fact that the root cause of our problems in life is a desire to control things. We want to control our life; we want to control other people's lives; we want to control our environment; we want to play God. We want to be at the center of the universe. But, when we try to do all of that, well, we just end up with fatigue, frustration, and failure.

Last Sunday we also talked about getting past the denial stage. But, what is denial really? Well, let me give you a picture. There once was a story printed in the lost-and-found section of a local newspaper. It said: Lost, a three-legged dog, blind in right eye, left ear missing, broken tail, recently castrated, answers to the name "Lucky." Now there's a good picture of denial.

Seriously though, denial is not a good thing. We need to get past that stage; we need to realize that we are not God and that we don't have control over the universe. That's the first step to recovery and the second step begins with the second letter of the word R-E-C-O-V-E-R-Y: "E," which stands for Earnestly believing that God exists. That I matter to Him, and that He has the power to help in all situations. This step is based on Hebrews 11:6, which says: *"Anyone who comes to God, must believe that He exists and that He rewards those who earnestly seek Him."*

The second step is what I call the Hope step. Step 1 says: I admit that I'm helpless, that I'm powerless. But step 2 says: There is a power. There is a power that I can plug into to help with the things that I can't handle on my own. Now, there are three parts to the Second step, to plugging into God's power. The first is this, Acknowledge that God exists. Probably, most of you have no problem with acknowledging that God exists. There aren't many atheists left anymore in this country. Gallup did a survey recently that said: 96% of the people in America say: "I believe in God." And less than 2% say: "I'm an atheist." There are far fewer atheists today than there were fifty years ago. I'm not quite sure why that is, but it's a good thing.

Acknowledging that God exists is the first part to plugging into God's power and the second part is to, understand God's character. A person must, not only acknowledge that God exists, but they must also have a good understanding of God's character. What's God really like?

This is very important because until we know what God is like, how can we trust Him? I'm not going to trust something that I don't know anything about. The good thing is that God wants us to know what He is like. He came to earth 2000 years ago in the person of Jesus Christ. And He said this is what I am like. We can know what God is like by looking at Jesus. In the first chapter of Paul's letter to the Colossians, he writes: *Christ is the visible expression of the invisible God. If you want to know what God is like just look at Jesus.* If you're reading about Jesus and studying His life well, you are on your way to learning a whole lot about God.

Here are three very important distinctions of God's character: First, God knows all about my and your situation. He knows the good and bad. Some of you may have had a tough week or month or life. But, look at what the Bible says. The Psalmist writes: *"You know how troubled I am O God. You've kept a record of my tears."*[91] Isn't that incredible? God knows us so well that He has kept a record of our tears. Now, you may say: "Nobody knows the pain I'm going through right now." Well, you're wrong, because God knows. God knows. Someone else might say: "Nobody knows how I'm struggling to break this habit, but I can't get it out of my mind." God knows. Or you might think: "Nobody knows the depression and the fear that I'm going through." But God does. God knows it all. Nothing escapes His notice. God sees the crisis in your soul right now and He is aware of all your needs even better than you are aware of them. God knows all about my and your situation and God cares about my and your situation. God knows what we're made of, dust. He knows that we are frail and that we are not super human beings.

God says: *"I have loved you with an everlasting love."* How can that be? How can God love me and how can His love never quit? How can He love me on good days and bad days, when I serve Him and when I don't, when I'm right and when I'm wrong? How does He keep on loving me? Well, you see, God is capable of loving with an unconditional love. God's love is not based on our performance, like human love, many times is.

God knows all about my and your situation, God cares about my and your situation. And, God can change any situation, even if that means change within us, within you or me. That's good news. God can change me and my situation. Sometimes He changes me, sometimes He changes the situation. Sometimes He changes both.

The apostle Paul wrote: *"I pray that you will begin to understand how incredibly great God's power is to help those who believe Him."* Do you ever find yourself paralyzed by procrastination? God says: "I've got the power." If God created each one of us, well, He can certainly help us with any hurts, habits or hang-ups that come our way. Nothing is impossible with God. And so, that situation that seems hopeless, well it isn't.

Okay, what are the three parts to the second step to recovery? Well, first we acknowledge that God exists. Second, we understand God's character. And third, we accept God's help. It's not enough just to believe in God. You've got to plug into God's power. Did you know that God is at work within you? He is, Philippians 2:13 says: *"God is at work within you, giving the will and the power to achieve His purpose."* In other words, willpower on your own is not enough. Good intentions are not enough. You need God's will and God's power working within if you want to experience His abundant life in this lifetime. Now, you may be saying: "I don't even know if I want to change. I don't know if I want God's power working within me. Or I'm scared of change." Well, really all you have to do is pray: "God, I'm willing to be made willing." Let's say that together: God, I am willing to be made willing. What happens when we open up our lives to God? Well we hear in scripture that: *"The Spirit that God gives us fills us with power, love and self-control."*

That's what I want in my life. First, I want power in my life. I want power to do the things that I know are right. I want power to break free from the past and let certain memories go. I want power to get on with the kind of life God wants for me.

Then I want love. I want real love. I want to be able to love people and have them love me with an unconditional love. I want to be able to let go of hurts, so any walls that have been built up, between myself and others, will come down. I want a Christ-like love and I want a self-control that is controlled by Christ.

You know, you are not really in control until Christ is in control of your life. And it is only then that you will be able to understand what it means to "have it all together." Maybe that will be a first for you, because before, you were trying to pull yourself up by your own bootstraps, instead of relying upon God's power in this life.

How do we plug into God's power? Real simple, we not only believe, but we also receive. First, I believe that God exists. I believe that He knows and cares about my situation. I believe that God has the power to help me, and then I receive Him into my life; I ask that Jesus Christ put His Spirit within me. You do that by using a four-letter word. Let me spell it out for you, H-E-L-P.

Now, this Road to Recovery is not an easy one. It means facing up to some real problems that maybe you haven't wanted to deal with in a long time. It means taking some risks. It means being honest with yourself. It means trusting God. But, you know what? God says: "I will be with you." *When you go through deep waters and great troubles I will be with you God says. You won't drown. When you walk through the fires of oppression, you won't be burned up.*[92] God says: I will be with you this next week; I will be with you next month; I will be with you next year; I will always be with you, especially when you decide to face those issues that you have been afraid to face before.

Where are you hurting today? Are you going through some deep waters? Do you feel like you're going under for the last time? Are you going through the fire right now? Do you feel like you're stuck in a rut where all you can say is: "I feel so powerless?" Well, there is a Higher Power that you can plug in to. His name is Jesus Christ. I invite you to open your heart and your life to Him today. God's help is there for the asking, you only need to receive. Let's take a few moments of silence to go to the Lord and ask that He help us to receive what He has for each of us this day. Amen.[93]

Letting Go

<u>Matthew 11:28–30</u>
"Come to me, all you that are weary and are carrying heavy burdens and I will give you rest. Take my yoke upon you, and learn from me; for I am gentle and humble in heart, and you will find rest for your souls. For my yoke is easy, and my burden is light."

Did you hear the story about a pet-store delivery truck driver who was going down the road, and at every stop light he would run to the back of the truck, grab a 2 X 4 and start hitting on the side of the truck? Well, the guy next to him watched for a while and then asked: "What are you doing?" And the truck driver said: "This is only a two-ton truck and I'm carrying four tons of canaries. I've got to keep two tons of them in the air at all times."

Have you ever felt that your life was sort-of like that, tying to keep it all up in the air so that it won't come crashing down around you? You know, sometimes we human beings have a tendency to try and keep too many plates spinning at one time. We do that with life. We do that in relationships. We do that with habits. We get stuck with certain plates that we feel we just have to keep spinning. We get stuck in grief when we lose a loved one. We get stuck in anger when someone hurts us. We get stuck in our work, or maybe in an unhealthy relationship. And then we feel that we can't get out, and it becomes a vicious cycle. And once you get stuck, then you might start feeling guilty that you're stuck. Then you get afraid that you will always be there. Then, finally fear turns to depression and you begin to throw pity parties for yourself. And you resign by saying: "I give up. I can't change." And then the cycle only gets worse.

So, how does a person break out of a cycle like that? Well, that's what we've been talking about for a couple of weeks now. Step 1 is the admit step, I've got a problem, it's the reality step. Step 2 is the Hope step, which says: Not only am I powerless but God has power and He is willing to help out. He knows my problems and cares about my problems, and cares about me. He knows everything going on in my life. And He's offering to help me to change.

But it's not just enough to know that God will help you. You've got to take action. You've got to make a decision. You've got to walk across the line. So, in Step 3 we consciously choose to commit all of our life and will to Christ's care and control. This step is based on Jesus words recorded in Matthew 11, one of my favorite passages where He says: *Come to Me all who are weary and are carrying heavy burdens and I will give you rest. Take My yoke upon you and learn from Me for My yoke is easy and My burden is light.* Jesus says: *"Come to Me."* It's God's invitation to us. He says: I will make your life easier. I will lighten your load. You will have rest and rejuvenation. Allow Me to control and care for your life and then, watch what I can do. Sounds easy, doesn't it? But, there are things that can keep a person from taking this third Step.

Here are five of them. Pride will keep me from admitting I need help. Proverbs 18:12 says: *"Arrogant people are on the way to ruin because they won't admit it when they need help."* And Proverbs 10:8 says: *"The self-sufficient fool falls flat on his face."* If you are not yet ready to give control of your life to Christ, well watch out because God does have a way of getting the attention of a person who believes that he or she is self-sufficient.

Guilt will also keep you from taking this step. You may be ashamed to ask God to help you. Ever felt that way? I'm ashamed to look up? I don't want to ask God for help? Well, you are wrong in thinking that way, because there's no Sin that God will not forgive. Don't let pride or guilt keep you from taking this important step.

Fear will keep you from taking this step, too. I'm afraid of what I might have to give up. Have you heard the story about the guy who falls off a cliff and half way down he grabs a branch? He's hanging on for dear life. Five hundred feet down. Five hundred feet up. And he cries out: "Somebody help!" Then he hears the voice of God: "This is the Lord, trust Me, let go and I'll catch you." And he looks back down, the five hundred feet down and he looks up and says: "Is there anybody else up there?" You may be hanging on for dear life by that branch and saying: "Oh, this isn't so bad. No problem, really, I'm okay." Or you might say: "I don't want anybody controlling me." But, who are you kidding? You're being controlled all the time: You're controlled by the opinions of other people. You're controlled by hurts you can't forget. You're controlled by habits, and hang-ups, or by the way your parents brought you up. Do you know what freedom is? Freedom is choosing who controls you. When you give your life, the care and control of your life to Christ, He will truly set you free. Bob Dylan used to say: "You're going to have to serve somebody, even if it's your own ego." Real freedom is choosing who your master will be. When you take this Third Step, giving your life and will to God, you've never had it so good, because God takes what you've given Him, turns it around, adds new meaning, new significance, new vitality and then gives it back to you in a whole new way. Don't worry about the specifics of what you might have to give up. Just come to God saying: "God I don't even know what I want to give up, but I do know I want my life to be under your control." Then let Him take care of the rest. You will be amazed at what God can do.

Worry, can keep you from surrendering your life to the care and control of Christ. Sometimes we confuse the decision-making phase with the problem-solving phase. Back in 1963 when J.F.K. announced publicly, "We're going to put a man on the moon by the end of the decade," that was the decision. Had all the problems been solved when he made that decision? No.

If you're a good manager you know you never confuse decision making with problem solving. If you confuse them, you never make the decision. You have to make the decision then solve the problems later. Kennedy said: "We're going to go to the moon," then it was NASA's problem to figure out the solutions. Likewise, you just say: "God, I don't understand it all, but I want You to come into my life. If You can give me a better life than the one I'm living right now, I want it." It's amazing what God can do in a persons' life. Don't let worry keep you from making a decision for God.

Okay, this is the most important thing I'll say today: The Christian life is a decision followed by a process, same with recovery. It is a decision followed by a process. All that we're talking about today is the decision part.

You know, if you are going to take over an island, you have to start with a beach head. That's the way the military does it. When you make the decision to take this third step, what's happening is God gets a beach head in your life. The Bible calls it conversion or being born again. It just means God gets a presence in your life. Does that mean everything in your life is going to magically be perfect? Absolutely not, it just means God's in your life now, in a different way. He's got a beach head and, for the rest of your life He's going to be setting you free, little by little by little. It's a process. John Wesley called it sanctification. The process is God's work, just trust God with the process. God says: *"Cast all your anxiety on Me because I care for you."* He says, "I care for you. I hold you in My hand." And as you trust God remember Paul's words to the Philippians when he said: *"God who began a good work in you, will keep right on helping you to grow in His grace until His task is finally complete."*[94] Going on to perfection as Wesley would put it, is God's work.

Finally, doubt can keep you from taking this step. "I want to believe but my faith just seems so small." You know, it's not the size of your faith that matters. A little faith even the size of a mustard seed, the Bible tells us is enough. A little faith, in a big God, gets big results.

Okay. How does a person take this step? I accept God's Son as my Savior. I need to be saved. I need help. I realize I need God in my life. It means committing as much of myself as I understand at this moment, to as much of Christ as I understand at this moment. I accept God's Word as my standard for living. From now on I've got a manual that I'm going to live my life by. It's called the Bible. God says this is our standard by which we can evaluate life around us. *"All Scripture is inspired by God and useful for teaching the faith and correcting error for resetting the direction of a person's life,"*[95] the apostle Paul says. I accept God's will as my strategy, as my goal in life. You know, it's a good thing to begin every day by saying: "Lord, you woke me up this morning. That obviously means you have another day for me, a purpose for my life. So, what do You want me to do with it?" Not, what do I want to do, but what do You want me to do with it, God? If you will honestly and sincerely dedicate each day to God, well, I think that you just might be surprised at how quickly God's plan will become your plan or strategy for life.

I accept God's power as my strength. Philippians 4:13 says: *"I can do everything God asks of me with the help of Christ who gives me the strength and power I will need."* No longer do I have to rely on my own energy. You know, things just work a lot better when they're plugged in, and when you get plugged into God, you're not so tired all the time. Because God promises: *"I will give you My power to be all I want you to be,"* if you will just let Me.

Jesus says: *"I stand at the door and knock. If anyone hears My voice and opens the door I will come in and fellowship with them."* Jesus says: "I'm standing at the door of your life and I'm knocking and I'm saying I want to come into your life." Are you ready to open that door? You see, He's a gentleman. He's not going to beat the door down. Step Three means that you have to open the door. And the key that unlocks that door is willingness, not will-power, but willingness to accept God's power in your life, to go by His controls and His system.

Pilots fly by one of two ways, either by I.F.R. (Instrument Flight Rules) or V.F.R. (Visual Flight Rules). Every pilot flies by one or the other. I.F.R. is when you taxi out on a runway, go over to the control tower and submit to the controls of the system. You set your instruments, and it's a done deal. You are controlled by the instruments, which, I understand is a very safe way to fly. But with V.F.R. you just kind of taxi on the runway, look around and if it looks Okay you take off. With V.F.R. you just fly around and use your sight. V.F.R. is fine as long as you can see everything, when it's a clear day and there's not a lot of traffic. But one day, if you fly enough you're going to eventually hit bad weather. You're going to get lost in some clouds and you are going to have to pick up the microphone and say: "I need to switch over to I.F.R." Now, you may have done okay so far in life flying V.F.R. but there will come a time when you will inevitably experience bad weather. You will probably recognize the bad weather as pain in your soul, or maybe just an empty feeling, a feeling that something is just not quite right, or that something is missing from your life. At that point it is very advisable that you pick up the microphone and switch to God's system, that's the best way to avoid disaster.

The prophet Jeremiah wrote: *"I know the plans I have for you, says the LORD, plans for your welfare and not for harm, to give you a future with hope."*[96] A future with hope, that's what God desires for you, that's what God offers to you when you make the decision to switch over to God's system, when you consciously choose to commit all of your life and will to Christ's care and control.

What more can I say, a future with hope, submit to Him; submit your life to God. Let go of anything that is keeping you from doing that and, then you will have a glorious future with hope. So be it. Amen.[97]

Confession, Good for the Soul

<u>1 John 1:5-2:2</u>

This is the message we have heard from him and proclaim to you, that God is light and in him there is no darkness at all. If we say that we have fellowship with him while we are walking in darkness, we lie and do not do what is true; but if we walk in the light as he himself is in the light, we have fellowship with one another, and the blood of Jesus his Son cleanses us from all sin. If we say that we have no sin, we deceive ourselves, and the truth is not in us. If we confess our sins, he who is faithful and just will forgive us our sins and cleanse us from all unrighteousness. If we say that we have not sinned, we make him a liar, and his word is not in us. My little children, I am writing these things to you so that you may not sin. But if anyone does sin, we have an advocate with the Father, Jesus Christ the righteous; and he is the atoning sacrifice for our sins, and not for ours only but also for the sins of the whole world.

For the last three weeks, we've been looking at how to handle hurts, habits, and hang-ups, that have found their way into our lives. We've taken the word "Recovery," each week, and looked at each letter as it represents one of the eight steps that will help us get away from the things that cause difficulties in our lives.

The first week we talked about the Reality Step: Realize I'm not God, that I'm powerless to control certain tendencies, and that I have problems I can't control. The next week we talked about earnestly believing that God exists, that I matter to Him, and that He has the power to help me. And last week we talked about commitment. It's not enough to know that I've got problems and that God can solve them, but I must consciously turn them over to Him. I must commit my life and will to God, saying: "God, here is my life, the good, the bad and the ugly. Everything, I give it to You." And today, we are on the letter "O" in the word recovery, which stands for this: Openly examine and confess my faults to God, to myself, and to someone I trust.

Let us pray: May the words of my mouth and the meditations of each of our hearts be acceptable in Your sight, O God, our Rock and our Redeemer. Amen.

Step Four, is the Housecleaning Step. It has to do with cleaning up the past, letting go of guilt, gaining a clear conscience, and learning to live the way God wants us to. Now, why you might ask, is this a part of the process? Well, because guilt is not a good thing. There are consequences to guilt. First, guilt destroys a person's confidence. You can't be confident with guilt in your life. It makes you feel insecure; it makes you worry saying things like: "What if somebody finds out who I really am. What if they reject me?" And no one wants to be rejected, because rejection hurts. Guilt whittles away at our confidence, until it is all gone.

Many years ago Sir Arthur Conan Doyle, writer of the Sherlock Holmes novels, was quite a prankster, and one day he decided to play a trick on five very prominent men in England. He sent an anonymous note to each of these five men and that simply said: "All is found out, flee at once." And, within twenty-four hours all five men had left the country. Guilt has a way of robbing a person of their confidence. It's not a good thing.

Second, guilt damages relationships. Guilt can cause us to respond to people in the wrong way. Guilt can make us impatient with other people. Guilt can cause us to overreact in anger. Sometimes the persons themselves don't even know that it was guilt that caused them to act that way. Guilt can also cause us to over-indulge other people. Parents often feel guilty and so they over-indulge their children by giving them lots of material things. Guilt can cause us to avoid commitment in a relationship. A lot of marriage problems today are caused by guilt over things that happened many years earlier.

First, guilt destroys confidence; second, it can damage a relationship. And third, Guilt keeps us stuck in the past. Living in the past is sort of like driving forward, while looking in the rear-view mirror. If you do that too long, you are probably going to crash. You can't go through life, always looking into the rear-view mirror. Guilt replays in a person's mind, over and over and over, the things they wish they could change. But, you know what? Guilt can't change the past any more than worry can change the future. Instead, it just makes today miserable and can even make a person sick. Psychiatrists say that seventy percent of the people in mental hospitals could leave today if they knew how to resolve their guilt. This is a very important step.

So, how do you do this step? Well, the procedure is quite simple; it just requires a lot of courage. The psalmist wrote: *"What happiness for those whose guilt has been forgiven. What relief for those who have confessed their sins and God has cleared their record."*[98] First, take a personal moral inventory. What that means is that you get alone by yourself. You get a pencil and a notepad and you sit down and say: "What is wrong with me? What have I felt guilty about? What have I regretted? What have I felt remorseful about? What are the faults in my life that I know need changing?" And then you ask God to help. You ask God to bring to your mind the things you consciously feel guilty about, and the things you unconsciously feel guilty about.

This is very biblical, actually. Lamentations 3:40 says: *"Let us examine our ways and test them."* God says we need to examine our lives, as well as, ask for His guidance. King David understood that when he prayed: *Search me O God, and know my heart. Test my thoughts, point out anything You find in me that makes You sad.*[99]

Now, when you take this moral inventory, you need to take your time and not rush. Take whatever time you need to get it done, but get it done. It's important. And do it in writing. Why? Well, because it forces you to be specific. Thoughts disentangle themselves much better when they pass through the lips and the fingertips. That means, I've thought about it, I can say it, and I can write it down, I've really got it clear now. If you can't do that, well, it's still too vague. You can't just say: "God, I've blown it in life." We all know that. No, specifically, you need to write it down. That will help you face reality and avoid getting stuck in the denial stage.

The first part is that of taking a moral inventory. You sit down and write out what's bugging you, how have you bugged others and what are your faults, your sins and your mistakes. After you've taken a personal moral inventory, you then accept responsibility. Say: I accept responsibility for my faults. Proverbs 20:27 says: *"The Lord gave us a mind and a conscience. We cannot hide from ourselves."* The greatest holdup to the healing for my hang-ups is me. The greatest holdup to the healing for your hang-ups is you. We've got to be able to say honestly to ourselves: "I'm the problem." And not say: "If I just change relationships, if I just change jobs, if I just change towns, then everything will be all right." No, we have to accept responsibility for our part in the problem. And don't rationalize, saying: "Oh, it happened a long time ago, or it's just a stage, or everybody does it." And don't minimize, saying: "It's no big deal." And don't blame others either, thinking: "It's mostly their fault." You know, it may be mostly their fault, but God holds you responsible for the ten percent that's your fault.

Take responsibility for your part. Scripture tells us: *"If we claim to be without sin, we deceive ourselves and the truth is not in us."* The point is that if I really want to win, I've got to stop deceiving myself. And pretending that it's everyone else's fault, instead of my own, is deceiving myself. What are you pretending to not feel guilty about, but in your heart you still do? Don't you think it's time that you finally dealt with it, so you can get on with the good things in life?

Okay, you take a moral inventory and then you look at the list and say: "Yes, that's me. I accept responsibility for my faults." And then, third, I ask God for forgiveness. First John 1:9 says: *If we freely admit that we have sinned we find God completely reliable. He forgives our sin and makes us thoroughly clean from all that is evil.* If we freely admit our faults, God will forgive us. What is the right way to ask God for forgiveness? Well, you don't beg. You don't bargain, and you don't bribe, you just believe. You believe that God will forgive you. When we freely admit that we have sinned, we find God completely reliable. He forgives our sin and makes us thoroughly clean from all that is evil. You just say: "God, You're right, it's wrong." That's what it means to confess. It just means to say: "God, You're right, it's wrong." Confession is agreeing with God, pure and simple. And also remember that there is absolutely no Sin that is too bad or too great for God to forgive. Just come humbly before Him and ask for His forgiveness. That's all that's required. The prophet Isaiah wrote speaking for God, saying: *No matter how deep the stain of your sin, I your God can take it away and make your life as clean as freshly fallen snow.*[100] That's the soap-bar verse. God says: *"No matter what the stain is, I can remove it."*

Fourth, I admit my faults to another person. God says it is absolutely essential for healing. In James we hear: *"Admit your faults, to one another and pray for each other so that you may be healed."*[101] How are we healed by admitting our faults to one another? Why do I need to drag another person into this? Why can't I just admit it to God? Well, because the root of the problem is relational.

We lie to each other. We deceive each other. We are dishonest with each other. We hurt each other. We wear masks. We pretend we have it together. But we don't. And all of this isolates us from others. It is the revealing of your feelings that begins the healing process. It's amazing, when you risk honesty with one person, a wonderful feeling of freedom will come into your life. You admit your faults to one other person. Everybody needs one. You don't need more than one, but you need at least one person you can be totally honest with. There is something therapeutic about this. It's God's way of freeing us.

Now, do I just go out and broadcast my sins to everybody? No. Telling the wrong person could be big trouble. No, instead you find someone you trust. You find someone who can keep a confidence, who is not a gossip and who has a reputation of confidentiality. You find someone who understands the value of what you're doing. You find someone who is mature enough that they are not going to be shocked when they hear that you are not perfect. It is also important that they know the Lord well enough, so that they can reflect His forgiveness for you. This may be a close trusted friend, or a Christian counselor.

Then, what do you say? You find a safe place and take your moral inventory list and say: I just need somebody to listen to me as I take my fourth step in this process. Here's some things I know are wrong in my life, this is what I've done, this is what I've felt. And when you find someone who will listen with forgiveness, well be prepared to experience relief like you've never experienced it before. All of a sudden the secret that's been making you sick cannot make you sick any longer, because it's not a secret anymore. Remember, be specific. The secret you want to conceal the most is the one you need to reveal the most, because that's where you need to experience God's grace the most.

When do you do this sharing? Well, as soon as possible. Don't procrastinate. But, you might be saying: I am just not so sure I am ready to take this step. Well, that's okay too; you just need a little more pain to get you there. And once you're ready you will take this step. But, my advice is this: Try to find that trusted person to share your personal moral inventory with, as soon as possible.

And finally, the last part is to: Accept God's forgiveness and to forgive yourself. Now, some of you may be thinking: "Pastor you planned this sermon for me." But, really, I didn't. We're all in the same boat. Pastors need to take this step too. We're all in the same boat. We're just a bunch of sinners. Who are we trying to kid anyway? Nobody with the exception of Jesus Christ is perfect. We've all blown it. We've all made mistakes. It's not like anyone is more righteous than anyone else. We've all got problems, just in different areas. What happens when I take this step? How does God forgive? Well, God forgives instantly. He doesn't wait. The moment you do this, you're forgiven. He never makes us wait. God never makes us suffer for a while. Humans do that, but God doesn't do that. He also forgives freely. God freely takes away our sins. We don't deserve it; we don't earn it; we can't work for it. It's free. And, God forgives completely. He wipes the slate clean. Scripture tells us: *"There is no condemnation for those who live in union with Christ Jesus."* You know, it turns out that this confession thing really is good for the soul. Praise God. Amen.[102]

Making Changes

<u>Romans 12:1–2</u>
I appeal to you therefore, brothers and sisters, by the mercies of God, to present your bodies as a living sacrifice, holy and acceptable to God, which is your spiritual worship. Do not be conformed to this world, but be transformed by the renewing of your minds, so that you may discern what is the will of God--what is good and acceptable and perfect.

We all have hurts, hang-ups, and habits that are messing up our lives. And if we are wise we will (at some point) throw our hands into the air and say: "Jesus take the Wheel," 'cause we can't do life on our own. Today we are going to talk about how we can with God's help, make changes in our lives. Imagine riding in a speedboat that has its auto-pilot set to go east, while you have decided to go west. Well, you have two possible ways to do that. One way is to grab the steering wheel and physically "force it" to head in the opposite direction. By sheer willpower you could overcome the auto-pilot, but your arms would eventually get tired, you'd let go of the steering wheel, and the boat would instantly head back east, the way it was internally programmed. That's what happens when you try to get rid of the hurts, habits or hang-ups in your life without God's help. Now it is true that willpower can produce short-term changes, but there will be internal stresses because you haven't dealt with the root cause. The change won't feel natural, so eventually you'll give up, go off your diet, quit exercising, go back to being unorganized, or start doing those things that you know are not good for you. But there is a second way that will work. Make the decision to change your auto-pilot from your willpower to God's power.[103]

Let us pray: May the words of my mouth and the meditations of each of our hearts be acceptable in Your sight, O God, our Rock and our Redeemer. Amen.

We've been in this series called the Road to Recovery for several weeks now, and today we're going to look at step 5, the Step that we will call transformation. It's the "V" in the word Recovery. Voluntarily submit to every change God wants to make in my life and humbly ask Him to remove my character defects. Today's message is based on Romans 12:1-2 which says: *"Offer yourselves as a living sacrifice to God, dedicated to His service and pleasing to Him, and let God transform you inwardly by a complete change of your mind."*[104] The way we are transformed is by having our mind changed. This morning I simply want to do three things. I want to talk about: Where character defects come from. Why it is so hard to get rid of them and how we can cooperate with God's change process.

So, where do character defects come from? Well, basically they come from three places. There's a biological source (my chromosomes), a sociological source (my circumstances) and a theological source (my choices). First, chromosomes, both your parents contributed to your 23,000 chromosomes. And so you inherited some of their weaknesses. We can inherit physical and emotional defects from our parents. This explains our predisposition towards certain problems. But it doesn't excuse Sin. For example, because of my parents, I may have a tendency to have a hot temper, but that doesn't excuse me to go out and murder somebody. Or I may have a tendency to be lazy, but that doesn't excuse me to do nothing with my life. Or I may have a tendency, genetically, to be given toward certain addictions, but that doesn't excuse me to go out and make the choice to become addicted. Our chromosomes, our genetics are one source of character defects.

Our circumstances are another. While we are growing up, we learn a lot of our ways of relating, our patterns, and our habits. We learn from our parents and we learn from other people. We learned to respond to our own needs in certain ways and how to cover for ourselves. A lot of our defects are simply self-defeating attempts to meet unmet needs. We all have a legitimate need for respect. But if we don't get respect early in life, we may settle for attention, and seek to get it in many various ways. We have a need for security but if we don't get it, we may have tried to cover ourselves with materialism and possessions to show that "I am secure."

Third, my choices can be a source of character defects. Simply this, if you choose to do something long enough, it becomes a habit. There may be something you never intended to develop in your life, but because you chose to do a certain thing long enough, it became a habit.

Okay, the second thing I wanted to talk about was: Why it takes so long to get rid of these defects in life? Well, first, because we've had them so long. We didn't get our defects overnight. It took years. Many of our habits, we developed in childhood, and here's the thing: They may not be comfortable and they may even be self-defeating, but at least they are familiar. It's like an old pair of shoes. Maybe they're not the best for running, but they are familiar. That makes them hard to let go of. It also takes a long time to get rid of defects because we identify with them. We confuse our identity with those things. We say: "That's just the way I am." When you say: "That's just the way I am" you're identifying with your defeat. Complete this sentence in your mind: "It's just like me to be what? A workaholic. Overweight. Anxious. Passive. Fearful or hot-tempered. The thing is, when you identify with a defect, it becomes a self-fulfilling prophecy. You say: "I'm always nervous when I get on a plane." And what's going to happen the next time you get on a plane? You're going to be nervous.

But, really what happens is that unconsciously, we're afraid that if we let go of our familiar defects, well somehow we won't be who we are. That means we change and sometimes change, sometimes the unfamiliar is just plain old scary.

Next, it is difficult to get rid of defects, because they have a payoff. Every defect has a payoff. It may mask my pain. It may give me an excuse to fail. It may allow me to compensate for guilt in my life. It may get me attention. A mother says to her kids: "Children, come down to dinner." And they don't come. So she yells: "Kids come down to dinner." And they come. This mom has figured out that if she yells, that's her defect, her children will come. And so she thinks: If I stop yelling at my children, will they still obey me, will I still be the authority figure in their lives?

Finally, it's difficult to get rid of defects, because Satan discourages us. Satan is constantly suggesting negative thoughts. He's the accuser. He says: "That will never work, you can't do it; you can't change." The Bible says however, that Satan is a liar. In fact is says that he is the father of all lies. You know, it is the truth; it is God who sets us free.

So, let's look at truth. How do I cooperate with God's change process in my life? Well, Romans 12 tells us to: *"Be transformed by the renewing of your mind."* If you want to change your life you've got to change the way you think, your mind has to be transformed. So, here are seven ways that will help in the transforming of our mind, seven ways to refocus our mind. First, focus on changing one defect at a time. Proverbs 17:24 says: *"An intelligent person aims at wise action but a fool starts off in many directions."* An intelligent person is specific. You've got to be very specific. "God, what is it I need to work on? Is it my anger, my anxiety, my tendency to want to control people, my workaholism, or my dishonesty that I need to work on?"

Go back and get your moral inventory list that you made this past week. Go down that list and say: "God which of these is damaging my life the most? And let Him start working on that one. You must work on one defect at a time.

Second, focus on victory one day at a time. Matthew 6:11 says: "Give us this month our daily bread." No, it says: *"Give us this day our daily bread."* Why? Well, because God wants to give us enough strength to change for one day, not for one week, one month, or for eternity. And so here's a good morning prayer: "Lord, just for this day, I want to be patient; just for this day, I want to think pure thoughts, instead of lust; just for this day, I don't want to lose my temper; just for this day, I want to be positive instead of negative." Matthew 6:34 says: *"Don't worry about tomorrow, each day has enough troubles of its own."* Rome wasn't built in a day. Character wasn't built in a day. And character defects won't be removed in a day, either.

Third, I focus on God's power not my power, not my willpower. You already know willpower isn't enough. In fact, depending on your own strength blocks recovery. But, here's the good news: *"We can master anything with the help of Christ who gives us strength."* So each day, pray: "Lord, I know I can't change on my own power, but I'm trusting in You to take away this defect." And then literally imagine God taking away your defect. What am I working on first, my temper? Well, here's what I'd imagine in my mind. I'd imagine taking my temper out and opening up the garbage can, putting it in the garbage can, putting the lid on the top, and setting the garbage can out by the curb. Then a garbage truck comes up that says: "God & Son, doing business with people like you for 2000 years." Jesus sends out one of His buddies, they pick up the garbage, they dump it in the truck and they crush it down. Then I see the truck turn around and speed away with my temper, as far as the east is from the west. That's what it means to visually think about giving our problems to God. Focus on God's power not you own willpower.

Fourth, focus on what you want, not on what you don't want. *"Fix your thoughts on what is true, and good, and right. Think about things that are pure. Think about all you can praise God for and be glad about,"* is what Paul wrote to the Philippians.[105] If you have surrendered all your life to the care and control of God, if you've invited Christ into your life, then, you are a new person. The old has passed away, you are a new person in Christ with a new identity. Your primary identity is now based on your relationship to Christ and not any defect you may struggle with. Focus on what you want, not on what you don't want.

Fifth, focus on doing good not feeling good. We hear in Galatians 5:16: *"If you're guided by the Spirit you will be in no danger of yielding to self indulgence."* Do the right thing; don't worry about feeling the right thing. Do the right thing even though you don't feel like doing it, because you know it's the right thing to do. Eventually your feelings will catch up with your actions.

Sixth, focus on people who will help, not hinder you in making positive changes. The right kind of people will help you. The wrong kind of people will hinder, or even prevent your recovery. The Bible tells us: *"Bad company corrupts good character."* In other words, if you don't want to get stung, you stay away from the bees. If you know what kind of people tempt you just stay away from them. On the other hand, the Bible also says: *"Two are better than one and a threefold cord is not easily broken."* When you have help from the right kind of person, if you fall they can help you up again. You know, a person can't recover on their own. They must be in a group, in a relationship. That's what Celebrate Recovery offers. Last week we talked about building a moral inventory list of the things we feel guilty about. I asked you to make a list of those things and admit them to yourself, to God and to one other person you trusted. Many of you had every intention of doing that, I am sure, but maybe you didn't. If you did, you are more than likely in relationship with an accountability partner. And, that is what the Celebrate Recovery ministry is all about. It gives us a great opportunity to be with others who can help us and not hinder us.

That's why we have been asking God to guide us in the start up of a Celebrate Recovery ministry, right here in this congregation.

Okay, finally seventh, focus on progress not perfection. Don't worry about perfection. Celebrate Recovery is a process. It's a decision followed by a process. And God who starts His work in you will bring it to completion. Remember the beach head illustration we had a couple of weeks ago? God establishes a beach head in your life like an island and the rest of the time He's taking over the island little by little? Some of you are thinking that God will only love you once you hit a certain stage, once you get to a certain level of perfection. Wrong! God loves you at each stage in your perfection and in your growth. God will never love you any more than He already does right now. He will never love you any less than He does right now.

A mother looks at her child and she doesn't expect her seven-year-old to act like a seventeen-year-old. He or she still makes messes, but the mom is pleased with the stage that her child is at right now. And God is pleased with your growth and my growth, too. It's the direction of our heart that matters most. So my challenge to you today is to say: "God I want to voluntarily submit to the changes You want to make in my life. And, so I humbly ask that You remove my character defects." You know, God won't start changing you until you are entirely ready for the change. That means voluntarily saying to God: I want You to be my auto-pilot, I want to be changed by Your power.

And then, miraculously, most miraculously, He will start working on your thoughts and your inmost self. He will begin to heal you from those things that are causing you to have hurts, habits and hang-ups. That's what will happen when you make the decision to change your auto-pilot from your own willpower to God's power.

This whole process is about giving our lives and our will over to God, so that He can remove our character defects so that He can take away those things that are hurting us. Now, I don't know about you, but that's what I want in every area of my life. Amen.[106]

END NOTES

[1] Doug Stewart, 'Class Act,' Smithsonian, Oct. 2001, pp. 106-113

[2] Copyright: ©1999 MercyMe

[3] Contributed Source: Time magazine, 1-24-2000, p. 18. Cited by Help 4 Sunday/Whirlwind Resources

[4] David Carr

[5] Mark 1:10

[6] Dr. Gary Nicolosi, Sermon' 'God's Chosen'

[7] Paul J. Nuechterlein, adapted from Lectionary Stories Cycle B, John E. Sumwalt, Lima, OH: CSS Publishing, 1990, pages 44-47

[8] Matthew 10:2-4

[9] Leslie Weatherhead

[10] John A. Stroman

[11] Brett Blair

[12] Dr. Bill Bouknight

[13] Thomas G. Long

[14] John 3:16

[15] Mark 12:30

[16] Mark 12:31a

[17] John 4:35-36

[18] Rev. John Baker

[19] Michael D. Powell

[20] 2 Corinthians 4:3-4

[21] 2 Corinthians 4:5-6

[22] Ephesians 5:15-16

[23] Esther 4:13-14

[24] Ephesians 5:15-16

[25] Matthew 5:14

[26] Ephesians 5:8

[27] John 8:12

[28] Donald B. Strobe

[29] John 15:5

[30] O. Garfield Beckstrand II

[31] John 15:12-16

[32] James W. Moore. HEALING WHERE IT HURTS, Nashville: Dimensions for Living, 1993, pp. 101-102

[33] King Duncan

[34] *Bits and Pieces*, October, 1991

[35] John 17:1*b*-2

[36] 1 John 1:10

[37] 1 John 4:2-3*a*

[38] John 17:11

[39] Genesis 1:27

[40] King Duncan

[41] Today in the Word

[42] John 1:1-3

[43] John 1:3-5

[44] John 14:6

[45] Philippians 4:13

[46] King Duncan

[47] E. Stanley Jones

[48] Lyle E. Schaller

[49] Five Practices of Fruitful Congregations, p 14

[50] Five Practices of Fruitful Congregations, p. 31

[51] Luke 10:25-37

[52] Romans 12:14-21

[53] United Methodist Hymnal, #616

[54] Melanie Aron, *Personal Sacrifice*

[55] Philippians 3:8

[56] Philippians 3:13-14

[57] Allen R. Bevere

[58] 2 Corinthians 8:1-5

[59] Philippians 4: 12, 13, 19

[60] Philippians 4:12

[61] Philippians by Fred Craddock, John Knox Press, 1985 p. 78

[62] Philippians 4:6-7

[63] 1 Thessalonians 5:16-18

[64] John 20:19-31

[65] John 20:22

[66] John 16:7

[67] John 14:26

[68] John 21:1-2

[69] John 21:25

[70] David Spangler, Everyday Miracles

[71] Genesis 3:15

[72] Hebrews 13:5

[73] Brett Blair

[74] Brett Blair

[75] Thomas E. Boomershine, STORY JOURNEY, Abingdon Press, 1988, pp. 67-68

[76] E. Carver McGriff, Lectionary Preaching Workbook: Cycle B, Lima: CSS Publishing

[77] Romans 8:14-15

[78] Romans 8:15

[79] Isaiah 1:18

[80] King Duncan

[81] Romans 8:15

[82] Romans 8:17

[83] Glenn McDonald

[84] Romans 8:2

[85] 2 Corinthians 5:17

[86] Romans 8:14-15

[87] Romans 8:12-13

[88] Isaiah 57:18

[89] Message based on Reverend Rick Warren's "The Road to Recovery" sermon #1

[90] A fabricated story

[91] Psalm 56

[92] Isaiah 43

[93] Message based on Reverend Rick Warren's "The Road to Recovery" sermon #2

[94] Philippians 1:6

[95] 2 Timothy 3:16

[96] Jeremiah 29:11

[97] Message based on Reverend Rick Warren's "The Road to Recovery" sermon #3

[98] Psalm 32

[99] Psalm 139:23–24

[100] Isaiah 1:18

[101] James 5:16

[102] Message based on Reverend Rick Warren's "The Road to Recovery" sermon #4

[103] Rick Warren, Life's Healing Choices, pp. 181-182

[104] Romans 12:1–2

[105] Philippians 4:8:

[106] Message based on Reverend Rick Warren's "The Road to Recovery" sermon #5